How to Do Business With NASA

How to Do Business With NASA

A Practical Guide for Entrepreneurs, Innovators, and Contractors

Jeff Nosanov, JD, LLM

BEP

BUSINESS EXPERT PRESS

Leader in applied, concise business books

How to Do Business With NASA:
A Practical Guide for Entrepreneurs, Innovators, and Contractors

First published in 2026 by
Business Expert Press, LLC
222 East 46th Street, New York, NY 10017
www.businessexpertpress.com

ISBN-13: 978-1-63742-930-3 (paperback)
ISBN-13: 978-1-63742-931-0 (e-book)

Business Expert Press Portfolio and Project Management Collection

First edition: 2026

10 9 8 7 6 5 4 3 2 1

EU SAFETY REPRESENTATIVE
Mare Nostrum Group B.V.
Mauritskade 21D
1091 GC Amsterdam
The Netherlands
gpsr@mare-nostrum.co.uk

Dedication

This book is dedicated to Dr. Jacklyn R. Green, the manager at NASA Jet Propulsion Laboratory (JPL), who helped me find my strengths in the space industry.

Description

NASA is one of the most admired institutions in the world—synonymous with exploration, innovation, and scientific achievement. But behind the headlines of Moon missions, telescopes, and Mars rovers lies a vast and dynamic ecosystem of private companies, research institutions, and entrepreneurs who help make those achievements possible. Doing business with NASA is not only possible—it is encouraged, and in many cases, essential to the agency's success.

This book is a practical guide to understanding how to navigate that ecosystem. Whether you're a start-up founder, a government contractor, a university researcher, or a seasoned aerospace executive, this book will show you how to position your organization to work with NASA—through contracts, partnerships, grants, and more. We'll demystify the acquisition process, highlight key entry points such as the SBIR/STTR program and Space Act Agreements, and offer real-world insights into proposal development, compliance, and strategic alignment with NASA's mission directorates.

More than a procedural manual, this book also explores the culture, language, and expectations of working with NASA. It draws on 15 years of firsthand experience winning contracts with the agency, consulting aerospace clients, and helping companies translate their capabilities into compelling offerings for one of the most selective customers on Earth—or off of it. NASA isn't just looking for rockets and satellites. It needs software, data, sensors, materials, AI, logistics, communications, and more.

This book is your launchpad. Let's explore how to get your ideas into orbit—by doing business with NASA.

Contents

Preface xi

Acknowledgments xiii

Introduction: From Moonshot to Marketplace xv

Chapter 1   The Way It Was 1

Chapter 2   How It Works Now 27

Chapter 3   How It Is 55

Chapter 4   How It Might Be 83

Chapter 5   Navigating NASA's Next-Decade Business Challenges 99

References 107

About the Author 113

Index 115

Preface

This book was written between February and May 2025. This period was a historic upheaval and change in American politics and administration. The day before this sentence was written, NASA had announced plans to fire 10 percent of its workforce, only to back down at the end of the day. It is not at all clear what NASA or even the U.S. government will look like at the time this book is published. However, the author believes that this is the ideal time to write a book that has equal parts factual and speculative, as the underlying motivation for this project was to imagine the ways that NASA could change.

Thank you for choosing this book. I wrote it because I believe I am relatively uncommonly positioned to speculate in an informed way about how NASA will change over the next few years, and to explore what will probably stay the same and what might not. I worked officially for the NASA JPL from 2010 to 2014. Prior to that, I had become the first person in the United States to earn an LLM degree in space communications law. My thesis work was on international traffic and arms regulation, which qualified me for my first job in regulatory compliance at JPL. I quickly learned that this was not what I wanted to spend my career doing, and so I began to explore other ways in which I could make an impact.

Thanks to my manager, Jackie Green, I was given the opportunity to work on space mission proposals, which turned out to be my sweet spot. Working in that area ultimately gave me broad exposure to how NASA works domestically and globally and led me to ultimately do everything from managing the development of an interstellar mission concept to being part of the delegation to the United Nations in 2011. I would later become an independent consultant and researcher between 2014 and 2024. I sat on panels at headquarters and Goddard Space Flight Center and managed the proposal for several missions at the Johns Hopkins University Applied Physics Lab.

When the government shut down in 2019, I made my first attempt at writing a book and self-published my first book about how NASA works. That book was a breakdown of the structure of NASA and how science missions, particularly, are selected for funding and flight. This book is different, it is about how one does business with NASA, how that business contributes to NASA's and ultimately the United States' goals in space, and how those arrangements might change under the current administration.

It is not an exaggeration to say that as of February 2025, it's not clear which federal laws will even be enforced anymore. This is especially true in government contracting, as the current administration is selectively enforcing federal acquisition regulations, such as conflict of interest, and so on, and Congress has not objected. In fact, earlier this week, the administration put out an executive order stating that the president and the Attorney General are going to be exclusively interpreting federal law. This is a novel legal theory. Hopefully, this book is not simply a memoir of a bureaucracy that once was. Perhaps a strange time to write about federal contracting procedures and rules, but here we are.

I joined NASA because there is no greater human endeavor in my mind than space exploration. It challenges us at every level and forces us to put our differences aside, think clearly, and be our best. Despite the politics involved, most of human space exploration has been a celebration of human ingenuity, spirit, and cooperation. Venturing further into space than the Moon will certainly require new levels of all of those things. If you have picked up this book, you probably already feel similarly inspired, and I want you to know that you can contribute without having a hard science degree. In fact, those with hard science degrees need the rest of us to make sure they can do their work, usually by providing budgets, resources, and equipment.

Once in a while, it can also help to question the things that are considered impossible. Nature always wins, but we don't know all the rules of the game just yet.

Acknowledgments

I want to acknowledge my wife Lauren who has always supported my crazy goals.

INTRODUCTION

From Moonshot to Marketplace

When President John F. Kennedy stood before Congress in 1961 and declared that America would land a man on the Moon and return him safely to Earth before the decade was out, NASA had a single, unambiguous mission. Everything—budgets, politics, engineering priorities, even the public's imagination—was aligned toward that goal. The Apollo Program became the embodiment of focus. Its deadlines were immovable, its objectives measurable, and its success undeniable. The space agency was a spearpoint aimed at the Moon, and it hit the target.

Half a century later, the landscape could not look more different. NASA's ambitions are still lofty—sending humans to the Moon again, establishing a presence on Mars, peering deeper into the cosmos—but its path is far less direct. The Artemis program, intended to return astronauts to the lunar surface, has already weathered shifting timelines, altered mission architectures, and changed political winds. Each administration brings new priorities: a Moon-first strategy becomes Mars-focused; Mars becomes "back to the Moon"; deep space exploration competes with Earth science, climate research, and robotic missions. The long-term roadmaps are revised so often that they sometimes resemble sketches on a whiteboard rather than fixed blueprints.

Yet within this turbulence lies the most significant opportunity in NASA's history for private industry. While the Apollo era was overwhelmingly a government-built effort, today's NASA is increasingly a buyer, not a builder. The agency now spends billions annually on services and hardware sourced directly from the commercial sector. SpaceX launches astronauts to the International Space Station; private companies build lunar landers; small businesses provide everything from mission software to specialized research instruments. NASA's budget, though modest compared to Apollo's peak, now channels more money than ever into contracts with companies that are large and small.

This shift—from centralized, in-house capability to a distributed network of commercial partners—is not a sign of weakness. It's a recognition that the future of space exploration will be built on collaboration, where NASA serves as anchor customer, technical authority, and risk-taker for ambitious missions, while industry innovates and delivers.

This book will show you how to navigate that landscape. Whether you're a start-up with a breakthrough technology, a mid-sized engineering firm, or a seasoned aerospace prime, NASA's evolving procurement ecosystem is full of openings for those who understand its processes and culture. You will learn how to read the agency's shifting priorities, position yourself for contracts, and build relationships that outlast political cycles.

The Apollo era gave us the first great moonshot. Today's era offers something just as remarkable: a chance for your business to help define the next one.

CHAPTER 1

The Way It Was

From NACA to Early NASA Partnerships (1950s–1960s)

The partnership between NASA and private industry dates back to the agency's very origins. Even before NASA was formed in 1958, its predecessor, the National Advisory Committee for Aeronautics (NACA), had a long history of collaboration with the aviation industry. NACA conducted fundamental aeronautics research and openly shared its findings with U.S. aircraft manufacturers, effectively boosting the entire industry's capabilities. This collaborative ethos set the stage for NASA's creation and early operations. When NASA was established in 1958 amidst the Cold War **Space Race**, it inherited NACA's facilities, expertise, and cooperative approach, but on a much larger scale focused on spaceflight. From the start, NASA recognized that achieving ambitious space goals would require extensive involvement of private contractors across aerospace, electronics, and engineering sectors.

Early Space Contracts—Project Mercury

One of NASA's first major programs, Project Mercury (1958–1963), provides a clear example of early industry collaboration. Lacking in-house production capability for human-rated spacecraft, NASA turned to American industry to design and build the capsules that would carry the first U.S. astronauts. In January 1959, NASA selected the McDonnell Aircraft Corporation as the prime contractor to develop and produce the Mercury spacecraft. The initial contract called for McDonnell to design and construct 12 Mercury capsules, with the understanding that changes and ground support equipment would be negotiated as the project evolved. This landmark contract—one of the first of the Space Age—demonstrated NASA's strategy of leveraging private sector engineering talent to fast-track development. McDonnell, and its network of over 4000 subcontractors, delivered the capsules that would successfully carry six Americans into orbit and jumpstart U.S. human spaceflight.

This early collaboration set important precedents. NASA established **"prime contractor"** arrangements, wherein a lead company was responsible for delivering a complete spacecraft or system, while NASA defined top-level requirements and oversaw progress. Contracts were typically **cost-plus-fixed fee**, reimbursing companies for allowable expenses plus a profit margin—an approach seen as necessary given the technical unknowns of early space projects. The U.S. political climate of the late 1950s strongly supported this government–industry partnership. The Sputnik crisis had galvanized political will (and funding) to catch up to the Soviet Union, and President Dwight D. Eisenhower's administration approved using private industry to develop U.S. space hardware quickly. The result was a flurry of contracts not only for Mercury capsules but also for rockets and ground systems, often leveraging technology developed by military programs. For example, Mercury's Redstone and Atlas launch vehicles were adapted from Army and Air Force missile programs, produced by companies such as Chrysler and Convair under government contract.

The Role of Industry in Early NASA Technology

From the outset, NASA's collaborations were not limited to spacecraft structures. They spanned multiple sectors—computing, materials, and more—reflecting the broad technological needs of space exploration. A notable example is NASA's influence on the emerging **microelectronics industry** in the early 1960s. The agency's demand for lightweight digital computers for guidance and control would prove pivotal. In 1962, NASA announced that the Apollo program's prototype guidance computer would use the new innovation of **integrated circuits (ICs)**, which were then barely a few years old. At that time, IC technology was in its infancy, with extremely low production volumes. NASA's decision, alongside similar moves by the Air Force, provided a crucial early market for semiconductor firms. By the mid-1960s, NASA was purchasing **up to 60 percent of all ICs produced in the United States**—ordering tens of thousands of chips, primarily from Fairchild Semiconductor, to ensure that the Apollo spacecraft had reliable onboard computers. One historian noted that "*demand from NASA and the Air Force gave a major boost to the fledgling semiconductor industry in the late 1950s and early 1960s.*" In this way, NASA's partnerships extended beyond traditional aerospace; its contracts for cutting-edge components helped spur advancements in computing hardware, a trend that would continue through later decades (for instance, NASA's adoption of early IBM computer systems for mission control and the Saturn V rocket's guidance).

Building the Workforce and Knowledge Base

Early NASA–industry collaboration was also about tapping external expertise and growing a skilled workforce. Many NASA leaders themselves had industry backgrounds. The agency's first administrator, T. Keith Glennan, came from both academia and private industry and believed in harnessing American industry's capabilities. Moreover, NASA's Space Task Group—the unit that managed Project Mercury—worked closely with contractor engineers, effectively functioning as an integrated team despite coming from different organizations. This integration was facilitated by co-location (NASA overseers stationed at contractor plants) and by establishing clear communication channels and technical standards. An example of industry providing critical expertise was in **heat shield materials** for reentry vehicles: NASA partnered with companies to develop new ablative materials that could protect Mercury and Apollo capsules. The **political and economic environment** of the early 1960s strongly favored such partnerships—the U.S. government was willing to invest heavily in space, and industries were eager for lucrative contracts and the prestige of contributing to national goals.

By the early 1960s, as NASA moved from Mercury into the Gemini program (which built two-man spacecraft, contracted again to McDonnell) and plans for a lunar mission accelerated, the template for government–industry cooperation was well established. NASA would orchestrate and fund ambitious projects, *private companies would build the hardware*, and together they would push technological frontiers. The stage was set for the greatest collaboration of the era—the Apollo program—which would dwarf all previous projects in scale and complexity.

Reaching for the Moon—Apollo and the Peak of "Big Iron" Industry Collaboration (1960s)

By the mid-1960s, NASA–industry collaboration had scaled up to unprecedented levels under the Apollo program. President John F. Kennedy's bold 1961 mandate to land an American on the Moon "before this decade is out" injected NASA with a singular goal and virtually unlimited national support. Achieving this goal requires what has been called *a nationwide enterprise* of government, industry, and academia. Indeed, Apollo became a showcase of American industrial capacity: at its peak, the program employed roughly **400,000 people and involved 20,000 companies and universities** as contractors or subcontractors. NASA Administrator James Webb orchestrated Apollo much like a wartime mobilization, enlisting the country's largest aerospace firms to build the mission's many components. This public–private undertaking not only produced staggering engineering feats on a tight timetable but also shaped procurement strategies and partnership models for decades to come.

Prime Contractors and Landmark Apollo Contracts

NASA's approach to Apollo was to divide the enormous project into major systems and assign each to a **"prime contractor"** through competitive bids. In July 1961, for example, NASA selected North American Aviation (NAA) as the prime contractor to design and build the Apollo Command and Service Module (CSM), the spacecraft that would carry astronauts to the Moon and back. The formal contract between NASA and NAA was signed on August 14, 1963, and was at the time **the largest single research and development contract in U.S. history**. Similarly, Grumman Aircraft Engineering Corporation was awarded the contract to develop the Lunar Module (LM)—the separate spacecraft that would ferry astronauts from lunar orbit to the Moon's surface and back. Other major contracts included the gigantic Saturn V launch vehicle: Boeing was responsible for the first stage (S-IC), NAA for the second stage (S-II), and Douglas Aircraft for the third stage (S-IVB), with Rocketdyne (a division of North American) building the powerful F-1 and J-2 engines. IBM was contracted to develop the Saturn

V's instrument unit (the rocket's brain), while MIT's Instrumentation Laboratory (under contract to NASA) developed the Apollo Guidance Computer (AGC). In short, Apollo's hardware was almost entirely built by private companies—**with NASA acting as architect, integrator, and overseer** of this vast supply chain.

The scale of these contracts was unprecedented. For example, the Apollo CSM contract with NAA ultimately ran to billions of dollars and involved thousands of workers at NAA's Downey, California plant. Grumman's LM contract similarly engaged an army of subcontractors— from propulsion to electronics—to produce the delicate lunar landers on Long Island, New York. Managing cost, schedule, and technical risk across so many entities requires new rigor in program management. NASA brought in experienced leaders, such as Maj. Gen. Samuel Phillips from the Air Force, to impose discipline. General Phillips, as Apollo Program Director, famously treated **"NASA contractors as cooperative partners"** in Apollo's success, but held them to high standards—"*When they failed to perform, he took swift action.*" One example was Phillips' 1965 internal report criticizing NAA's management of the Apollo space-craft effort. That frank assessment led to significant managerial changes in the company and sharpened performance. This illustrates a defining feature of Apollo-era partnerships: contractors were given tremendous responsibility and trust, but NASA closely monitored progress, ready to intervene to keep the Moon landing on track.

Technical Collaboration and Innovation

The Apollo partnership also drove innovation in multiple fields. The mission's daunting requirements prompted collaborative R&D in areas such as **computing, materials science, and systems engineering**. The AGC, for instance, was co-developed by NASA, MIT, and industrial contractors, and it was one of the first embedded digital computers to use ICs. NASA's early and bulk purchase of these ICs for the AGC and Saturn rocket systems provided the fledgling semiconductor industry with demand (as noted, NASA bought 60 percent of U.S. chips by 1965) and pushed manufacturers to improve reliability. In materials science, NASA contractors created new heat shield materials (Avcoat ablative resin for the Apollo capsule) and light-but-strong alloys for the Saturn V. These breakthroughs often emerged from a close partnership: NASA would set performance specs (e.g., a heat shield must survive 5,000°F reentry), and industry chemists and engineers (at North American, DuPont, etc.) would iterate designs, with NASA labs testing and validating them. The result was not only mission success but also commercial spinoffs—technologies proven in Apollo found later uses in aviation, electronics, and other industries.

Economic and Political Context

The Apollo industrial effort unfolded in a very supportive environment. Through the 1960s, NASA's budget climbed to nearly 5 percent of federal spending, reflecting bipartisan political commitment to beat the Soviet Union to the Moon. This ensured a steady flow of funding into contractor coffers—though NASA imposed strict cost controls internally, the **cost-plus contracting** model meant that companies were reimbursed for allowable costs, reducing their financial risk. Politically, NASA and contractors were astute in spreading work across many states and congressional districts. This was sometimes done quite deliberately; subcontracting was encouraged not just for technical reasons but to **"spread the footprint"** of Apollo spending. By engaging suppliers and labor in dozens of states, NASA helped build a broad base of political support for the program. As a contemporary observer quipped, if the Apollo Saturn V rocket had logos of all its builders on the side, *"there would have been no room for windows"*—a testament to how many companies contributed hardware and components. This coalition-building paid off in sustained congressional funding year after year.

The Apollo Moon landings of 1969 were the crowning achievement of this government–industry partnership. It had not been a traditional commercial transaction—as **Time magazine** later noted, Apollo's contractors essentially did *"work for hire,"* turning NASA's detailed designs into reality. NASA dictated requirements down to the nuts and bolts, and industry delivered, under NASA's close supervision, to meet those specs. This model succeeded for Apollo's crash program, but it was extremely expensive and involved heavy oversight. By the time Apollo ended (early 1970s), NASA and political leaders were asking whether this approach could be sustained, or if new partnership models were needed to control costs. But during the 1960s, the formula of generous funding, clear objectives, and all-hands cooperation among NASA and industry proved capable of accomplishing the "impossible." Apollo not only met its goal but also entrenched the idea that **public–private collaboration is integral to U.S. space endeavors**—a notion that would be revisited and reinterpreted in subsequent decades as constraints tightened.

Post-Apollo Adjustments—The Space Shuttle Era and New Partnership Challenges (1970s–1980s)

The successful Moon landings brought NASA immense prestige, but the early 1970s ushered in a period of retrenchment. With Apollo's end, NASA's budget was sharply reduced, and thousands of contractor jobs were cut as production lines shut down. The agency and its industry partners faced the challenge of redefining their relationship in an era of tighter resources and changing goals. The **Space Shuttle program**, initiated in the early 1970s, became the next centerpiece of NASA–industry collaboration. Unlike Apollo's disposable spacecraft, the Shuttle was conceived as a partially reusable system to make access to space more routine and affordable. This ambitious agenda required innovations in engineering and also new thinking in procurement and operations. During the Shuttle era (roughly 1972–2011 for development and flights), NASA's partnership with industry evolved—maintaining the fundamental prime contractor model but also encountering cost overruns, external pressures to **"commercialize"** space, and new roles for industry in operations and support.

Shuttle Development Contracts

In 1972, after a vigorous competition, NASA selected **North American Rockwell** as the prime contractor to build the Space Shuttle orbiter, the winged spaceplane component of the Shuttle system. This contract, awarded on July 26, 1972, was one of the largest of the decade—termed *"the biggest aviation contract in years"* at that time. Rockwell's win over rivals like Grumman and Lockheed was attributed not just to its technical design (which NASA rated highly, though Grumman's was considered slightly superior) but also to Rockwell's strong **management proposal empha-sizing cost control**. Memories of 1960s military programs that suffered cost overruns (e.g., the C-5 Galaxy) loomed large, and NASA was keen to see disciplined budgeting on the Shuttle. Rockwell, which had merged with NAA, brought Apollo heritage and promised a rigorous approach to managing development. The orbiter contract was valued in the billions and necessitated Rockwell to massively expand its workforce—the company's Space Division grew from 6200 employees to an expected 16,000 by 1975 in order to tackle the project. In a sign of the times, Rockwell explicitly planned to rehire engineers from the defunct Apollo programs, preserving human capital that might otherwise be lost.

Other major Shuttle elements were also contracted out: **Rocket-dyne** (by then part of Rockwell) for the reusable main engines, **Morton Thiokol** for the solid rocket boosters, and **Martin Marietta** for the huge external fuel tank. In each case, NASA followed a similar pattern as Apollo—defining the overall architecture and high-level requirements, then engaging industry to execute the detailed design and manufacturing. Contracts remained largely cost-plus, reflecting the significant technical uncertainties (the Shuttle's thermal protection tiles, for instance, were a novel challenge that led to delays and overruns). However, NASA imposed tighter oversight gates and milestone reviews to try to keep development within bounds. Despite these efforts, the Space Shuttle development ran over initial cost estimates and behind schedule—a reality that revealed limits of the Apollo-style contracting approach when budgets were con-strained. By the first orbital flight of **Space Shuttle Columbia** in 1981, the program's total development cost had roughly doubled from early 1970s projections. This strain forced NASA and contractors to continually justify the program's value to skeptical budget watchdogs. It underscored a need to balance innovation with cost realism in partnerships.

Industry Involvement in Shuttle Operations

A significant shift during the Shuttle era was the growing role of industry not just in building space hardware but also in operating it and providing services. In the initial years, NASA itself managed Shuttle launches and processing through its civil servant workforce and support-service contracts. However, following the Shuttle's entry to service, **pressure to reduce operational costs and encourage commercial use of the Shuttle** led to new partnership models. The **Commercial Space Launch Act of 1984** (enacted under President Ronald Reagan) encouraged private sector involvement in space transportation and directed NASA to transfer routine launch services to industry where possible. Reagan's vision was that the Shuttle would carry not only government payloads but also commercial satellites and even private citizens, ushering in a new era of **space commerce**. In practice, NASA began marketing excess Shuttle capacity to commercial satellite operators in the early 1980s, effectively acting like a launch service provider. Fees were initially kept low to attract business, which undercuts emerging private launch companies (like those developing expendable rockets). NASA's close partnership with industry in Shuttle operations evolved further with the creation of the **United Space Alliance (USA)** in 1996—a joint venture of Boeing and Lockheed Martin—which was contracted to handle day-to-day Shuttle processing and operations on NASA's behalf. This outsourcing was intended to streamline the program and cut costs by consolidating hundreds of separate contracts into one umbrella contract managed by USA. It exemplified a new kind of public–private arrangement: NASA as owner/customer of the Shuttle system, with industry as operator.

However, the Shuttle era also witnessed setbacks that affected NASA–industry dynamics. The **Challenger disaster** in 1986 halted Shuttle flights for two-and-a-half years and led to soul-searching about NASA's management practices and the limitations of the Shuttle as an "all things to all people" vehicle. In the aftermath, **policy changes** sharply curtailed the commercial role of the Shuttle. The Reagan Administration determined that NASA would no longer fly commercial satellites on the Shuttle once alternative rockets were available, to **"encourage a commercial launch industry."** This decision essentially ceded the launch of most commercial payloads back to expendable launch vehicles built by companies such as McDonnell Douglas, Boeing, and Martin Marietta (who later formed United Launch Alliance [ULA]). Thus, paradoxically, one effect of Challenger was to boost private launch providers—NASA stepped back from competing in the launch market, opening room for purely commercial services (albeit initially those providers were still using government-developed rockets). Additionally, studies after Challenger (including one led by Gen. Sam Phillips, who returned as a consultant) found that NASA's oversight of contractors had become too complacent; the Rogers Commission identified flawed communication between NASA and booster contractor Morton Thiokol regarding O-ring problems. In response, NASA tightened supervision on Shuttle contracts and reprioritized safety over schedule or market ambitions. The late 1980s saw NASA and its contractors implementing numerous safety upgrades and more rigorous risk management, reaffirming that while NASA relies on industry, the agency must maintain robust insight into technical decisions.

Broadening Industry Engagement

Despite the Shuttle program dominating NASA's human spaceflight in the 1980s, the agency also engaged industry in other sectors and initiatives. For example, NASA's **space science missions** (planetary probes, Earth satellites) continued the practice of contracting companies such as Lockheed, Boeing, Hughes, and IBM to build spacecraft and instruments. A notable trend initiated in the 1970s and expanding in the 1980s was NASA's use of **"Other Transaction" agreements** (enabled by the Space Act of 1958) for experimental projects. An early instance was the **Space Shuttle Main Engine** development in the 1970s, where Rocketdyne and NASA shared some risk; later, the **Space Station Freedom** effort (begun in 1984) explored contractor roles in system integration (ultimately awarded to Boeing, as discussed shortly). NASA also launched the **Space Shuttle Spacelab module** in partnership with the European Space Agency (ESA) and firms like McDonnell Douglas building the lab module—showing international industry partnerships.

The economic context of the 1980s—characterized by rising federal deficits and a political tilt toward privatization—influenced NASA's approach. The agency was encouraged to **"buy commercial"** where possible, meaning use off-the-shelf or commercially provided services rather than bespoke developments. One manifestation was NASA's purchase of commercially available computer systems and software (rather than custom-building everything as done in Apollo). Another was the **encouragement of commercial experiments** on Shuttle flights (companies could pay to fly materials processing experiments in orbit). While modest in scale, these steps indicated NASA's gradual openness to more market-driven collaboration, a theme that would greatly expand in later decades.

In summary, the Shuttle era saw NASA and private industry maintaining a close, though sometimes strained, partnership. Industry continued to be indispensable—designing, building, and even running the nation's flagship spacecraft. Yet, with budgets tighter than Apollo and with the Shuttle taking on multifaceted roles, cracks in the cost-plus-contracting model became evident. The tragedies of *Challenger* (1986) and later *Columbia* (2003) underscored that ultimate responsibility and risk remained with NASA, even as contractors performed much of the work. By the end of the 1980s, NASA was beginning to consider new ways to engage industry that could reduce government burden and invite more innovation, setting the stage for the transformations to come.

Toward a Space Station and "Faster, Better, Cheaper"— Industry Consolidation and New Approaches (1990s)

The 1990s were a decade of transition for NASA and its industry partners. With the Cold War over, both the political rationale and funding levels for space activities evolved. NASA's budget flat-lined or shrank in real terms through much of the decade, forcing the agency to seek more cost-effective methods. At the same time, the aerospace industry underwent **major consolidation**: companies that had been competitors in Apollo (such as McDonnell Douglas, Rockwell, and Grumman) merged into a few giant firms (Boeing, Lockheed Martin, etc.). This consolidation changed NASA's contractor landscape—by the late 1990s, NASA often had a single large prime contractor available for each major project, reducing competition. Against this backdrop, NASA pursued two significant endeavors: the building of the **International Space Station (ISS)** and the implementation of Administrator Daniel Goldin's philosophy of "faster, better, cheaper" for science missions. Both efforts further shaped NASA–industry collaboration, introducing new contract structures and partnership ideas, some successful and some cautionary.

Building the International Space Station

The ISS, conceived as Space Station Freedom in the 1980s and redesigned in the early 1990s to include Russia and other partners, became NASA's largest program after the Shuttle. In 1993, as part of a post-Cold War revitalization of the project, NASA selected **The Boeing Company** as the prime contractor for the ISS. Boeing's contract (formally beginning January 13, 1995, as a cost-plus-award-fee contract) made it responsible for integrating the many components of the station and building core elements such as the U.S. lab module and Node connectors. This award reflected Boeing's status as a merged entity of several Apollo-era companies—by 1993 Boeing had absorbed or partnered with Rockwell and McDonnell Douglas, bringing immense combined experience to the table. Boeing's role was so central that one ISS manager noted that over "a million drawings" for station parts bore Boeing or its heritage companies' logos, underscoring the company's deep involvement in design and construction.

The ISS contracting model was traditional in one sense (Boeing on cost-plus, with many subcontracts), but innovative in another—NASA sought to treat Boeing as an "*industrial partner*" responsible for end-to-end delivery, rather than micromanaging every interface. In practice, NASA still maintained tight oversight (the complexity of international partner contributions and safety requirements necessitated it), but Boeing was given significant latitude in vendor selection and technical solutions. Over the 1990s, as ISS assembly began, NASA and Boeing had to adapt to technical challenges (modules delivered late, cost growth) and geopolitical shifts (Russia's contribution and economic woes). Notably, a 1998 amendment to the Space Station contract converted much of Boeing's work to a **performance-based contract**, with incentives for controlling cost and meeting schedule—an attempt to mitigate the open-ended nature of cost-plus. The ISS experience taught NASA valuable lessons in managing a long-duration partnership: the importance of clear requirements definition (station redesigns caused churn), the need for independent verification of contractor analyses (to avoid optimistic assessments), and the value of sharing risk. Indeed, by the end of the 1990s, NASA began inserting contract clauses that put more responsibility on contractors to cover overruns or to achieve specific performance metrics for full-fee award.

"Faster, Better, Cheaper" and Diverse Partnerships

In the 1990s, NASA Administrator Dan Goldin popularized the slogan "faster, better, cheaper" to describe a desired shift in how NASA developed missions—especially smaller robotic science missions. This approach favored smaller contractors and innovative companies, aiming to break the pattern of huge, year-long projects in favor of nimble development. One outcome was the **Discovery program** of planetary probes, where NASA invited proposals from industry-led teams for cost-capped missions. This allowed smaller firms like Spectrum Astro and Ball Aerospace to win contracts for spacecraft like *NEAR Shoemaker* and *Deep Impact*, often with universities as partners. Though not in-human spaceflight, this broadened NASA's industry base and experimented with **fixed-price contracts** and **competitive procurements** for complete spacecraft. Companies were expected to co-invest or at least manage within a firm cost cap—a departure from cost-plus habits. The results were mixed: some missions succeeded brilliantly at low cost, while others (e.g., Mars Climate Orbiter/Polar Lander in 1999, which crashed due to metric/imperial units confusion) failed, prompting debate about whether "cheaper" had gone too far. Still, this era injected a new entrepreneurial spirit and foreshadowed later commercial partnerships.

NASA also tried novel partnerships for technology development in the 1990s. A prominent example was the **X-33 program**—an attempted public–private venture to develop a prototype reusable launch vehicle (RLV). In 1996, NASA awarded Lockheed Martin a contract to develop the X-33 demonstrator (with the expectation that Lockheed would later build a full-scale RLV, VentureStar, potentially for commercial use). Unlike a typical contract, this was structured as a **cooperative agreement** under NASA's Space Act: NASA and Lockheed would share development costs, and Lockheed would own the vehicle and intellectual property, potentially launching a commercial service. It was an early **public–private partnership** in launch development. Unfortunately, the X-33 program ran into technical difficulties (composite fuel tank failures) and was canceled in 2001 before flight, with neither party achieving the hoped-for outcome. The failure highlighted the risks when both government and company have skin in the game—Lockheed lost a considerable investment, and NASA gained little usable technology—but it also provided lessons that influenced the design of future partnerships (like clearly defining milestones and off-ramps).

By the late 1990s, NASA was laying groundwork for what would become the **commercial spaceflight revolution** in the next decades. In 1998, Congress passed the **Commercial Space Act**, which among many provisions directed NASA to explore using commercial providers for ISS cargo and encouraged the development of private space capabilities. NASA's **Johnson Space Center** initiated studies on "Alternate Access to Station"—essentially the idea of hiring commercial companies to deliver cargo to ISS as the Shuttle aged. Although funding at the time was limited, these studies kept alive the concept that blossomed into the Commercial Orbital Transportation Services (COTS) program a few years later. Another development was NASA's expanded use of **Space Act Agreements (SAAs)** in the late 1990s to partner with companies in early-stage tech development without the full formality of contracts. SAAs allowed more flexibility and less bureaucratic overhead, which some small tech firms found appealing when working with NASA.

Industry Consolidation Impact

The mergers forming Boeing and Lockheed Martin by 1998 meant that NASA increasingly dealt with single, large prime contractors for major systems. For instance, in the launch sector, Boeing's and Lockheed's launch divisions combined in 2006 to form ULA—a monopoly for U.S. government medium-heavy launches for a time. While this consolidation ensured a stable supply chain (from NASA's perspective, the big contractors were "too big to fail"), it also raised concerns about reduced competition and innovation. NASA began to look for ways to encourage new entrants. One small step in this direction was the **NASA Centennial Challenges** program, launched in 2005, which offered prize money for aerospace innovations (e.g., lunar lander analogs, space elevators) open to start-ups and nontraditional players. Though modest, it reflected a cultural shift: NASA was willing to pay for *results* rather than detailed plans, and to let anyone (not just traditional contractors) participate.

In summary, the 1990s saw NASA and industry maintaining their close ties through the massive Space Station project under a classic contracting approach, while simultaneously probing alternative models on smaller fronts. The lessons of this era—particularly from ISS contracting complexities and experimental partnerships—directly informed NASA's approach in the early 2000s. By 2000, with the Space Station nearing initial completion and the Shuttle facing eventual retirement, NASA was poised to try a radical evolution in its partnership model, one that would tap the growing commercial space sector for a new generation of vehicles.

The Rise of Commercial Spaceflight—COTS, Commercial Crew, and a New Model (2000s–2010s)

In the early 21st century, NASA's collaboration with private industry entered a new phase, often termed the **commercial era** of space. Two developments accelerated this shift: the impending retirement of the Space Shuttle (set for 2010–2011, after the ISS was completed) and the emergence of new private space companies with ambitious capabilities, most notably SpaceX (founded 2002) and Blue Origin (2000). NASA faced a strategic choice—build government-owned replacement vehicles for crew and cargo, or contract these services out to industry in a novel way. The result was a series of pioneering programs: **COTS** for cargo, **Commercial Resupply Services (CRS)** for operational cargo contracts, and the **Commercial Crew Program** for astronaut transport. These initiatives fundamentally changed NASA's procurement strategy, introducing *fixed-price, milestone-based payments*, and requiring industry to invest its own capital in development. The period from roughly 2005 to 2020 thus saw NASA move from the traditional contractor model to **public–private partnerships** that more closely resemble a venture investment or service acquisition.

Commercial Orbital Transportation Services (COTS)

Announced in 2006, COTS was NASA's groundbreaking program to stimulate development of private cargo vehicles to serve the ISS. Unlike previous contracts, COTS used **funded SAAs**—legal agreements under NASA's Space Act authority, not standard FAR contracts under the Federal Acquisition Regulations. This gave NASA flexibility to negotiate terms and share technical info without the full weight of federal procurement regulations. NASA set high-level requirements (deliver a certain amount of cargo to ISS, demonstrate safe reentry, etc.) but left design solutions to the companies. The agency allocated roughly **$500 million in "seed money"** for COTS, aiming to partner with two companies.[1] In August 2006, after a competitive selection, NASA signed agreements with **SpaceX** and **Rocketplane Kistler (RpK)**, awarding *SpaceX $278 million* and *RpK $207 million* in milestone-based payments through 2010.[2] The goal was for each to develop and test a new cargo spacecraft that NASA could then contract for ISS resupply. This was a **pay-for-performance** approach: companies received incremental payments only after achieving technical milestones that NASA had negotiated in advance (e.g., engine tests, flight demos). Notably, the companies had to cover any additional costs themselves—NASA's funds were a contribution, not the total cost. This leveraged private investment: SpaceX, for instance, reportedly spent well above the NASA contribution[3] to develop Falcon 9/Dragon, but in return it would own the system and could use it for other customers.

COTS had challenges. RpK struggled to meet early milestones and failed to secure enough private capital, leading NASA to terminate its agreement in 2007 (illustrating that NASA was willing to let a partner fail if performance lagged). NASA reallocated the remaining funds by bringing in a new partner, **Orbital Sciences Corporation**, in 2008, with an agreement worth about $170 million to develop the **Cygnus** cargo vehicle and **Antares** rocket.[4] Both SpaceX and Orbital ultimately succeeded in developing their systems, albeit on schedules about one to two years later than originally hoped. By 2010, SpaceX had the Falcon 9 launch vehicle flying, and in December 2010, the first Dragon capsule reached orbit and returned safely—the **first privately developed spacecraft to do so**. NASA's gamble was paying off: for a relatively small government investment, two new American launch systems were created. A **NASA analysis** later noted that the cost to NASA would have been several fold higher under a traditional contract; the agency's internal cost models

(NAFCOM) had estimated development of something like SpaceX's Falcon 9 by conventional means could range $1.7–4 **billion**, whereas SpaceX's actual development cost was on the order of only $300 million (their portion of COTS funds plus private money).[5] While not directly apples-to-apples, it demonstrated significant cost savings. As NASA's chief of Commercial Crew/Cargo at the time summarized, "*there were indications that a commercial approach offered significant cost savings to NASA.*"

From a partnership perspective, COTS was revolutionary. NASA acted more like an **investor and technical adviser** than a traditional overseer. The SAA framework meant NASA engineers could suggest and share expertise, but they did not direct every design detail—that was up to the companies. Additionally, NASA did not take ownership of the vehicles; the companies retained ownership and intellectual property, positioning them to offer services to customers beyond NASA. In effect, NASA helped Midwife with new commercial products. This aligns with a broader trend noted by NASA's chief economist in 2024: "*NASA has supported the commercial space sector for decades… developing new contract and operational models to encourage commercial participation and growth,*"[6] evolving from exception to a default method in the post-Shuttle era. COTS was a prime example of that philosophy in action.

From COTS to CRS (Operational Cargo Contracts)

In parallel with the final COTS demo flights, NASA moved to formal procurement of cargo delivery services, known as Commercial Resupply Services (CRS). In late 2008, NASA awarded the first CRS contracts to SpaceX and Orbital Sciences, totaling $3.5 billion for a series of delivery missions to ISS.[7] Under these **fixed-price contracts**, NASA essentially became a customer—paying per flight for a specified cargo upmass/downmass—rather than paying for vehicle development. SpaceX received a contract for 12 cargo flights (valued at about $1.6 billion) and Orbital for 8 flights ($1.9 billion).[8] These differing amounts reflected the companies' pricing and capabilities, but importantly, even $3.5 billion for a decade of ISS cargo was far cheaper than if NASA had to maintain the Shuttle or build a new fleet itself. The CRS contracts represented the fruition of the public–private model: NASA helped industry create capacity, and then **procured services at competitive prices**, creating a win–win. By 2012, SpaceX's Dragon became the first private spacecraft to dock with the ISS, and Orbital's Cygnus followed in 2013—tangible milestones that vindicated the COTS approach. NASA's Inspector General in 2013 noted that while NASA assumed some risks in the new model, the commercial cargo program had achieved its primary objective of multiple American supply lines to the ISS. It also highlighted NASA's need to monitor contractor schedules and performance (Orbital had some delays, leading OIG to urge NASA to adjust payment schedules to better align with progress). The oversight was less direct than in Apollo, but NASA still had to manage these partnerships to ensure mission needs were met.

Commercial Crew Program

Building on the cargo success, NASA turned into the even more crucial task of transporting astronauts. After the Shuttle's 2011 retirement, the United States relied entirely on buying seats on Russia's Soyuz spacecraft. To restore independent access to low Earth orbit (LEO), NASA initiated the Commercial Crew Program in 2010. It proceeded in phases: initial **Commercial Crew Development (CCDev)** rounds were SAAs with several firms to develop concepts (small awards to Blue Origin, Boeing, Sierra Nevada, SpaceX, etc.), followed by **Commercial Crew Integrated Capability (CciCap)** in 2012 (larger SAAs to three finalists: Boeing, SpaceX, and Sierra Nevada, to mature their designs). Finally, in September 2014, NASA made the major award of **Commercial Crew Transportation Capability (CCtCap) contracts to Boeing and SpaceX**, selecting them to finalize development, testing, and flight of crew capsules. The total award was **$6.8 billion**—$4.2B to Boeing for its CST-100 *Starliner* and $2.6B to SpaceX for its *Crew* Dragon.[9] This difference in amounts was based on each proposal's cost to meet NASA's requirements. Under CCtCap, NASA would pay each company to complete certification and perform at least one crewed test flight and then allowed for **up to six operational missions** for each to ferry astronauts to ISS. Importantly, unlike earlier phases that were under SAAs, these final contracts were **fixed-price, FAR-based contracts**. NASA shifted back to a traditional contract for the final stage to solidify commitments, but many commercial practices remained—including companies retaining ownership of their spacecraft and the ability to use them for non-NASA missions.

The Commercial Crew Program illustrated a hybrid of old and new partnership models. NASA set **high-level safety and performance requirements** (e.g., redundancy, launch abort capability, and rendezvous standards) but did not dictate design specifics. Boeing and SpaceX each contributed significant corporate funds (especially SpaceX, whose total development cost exceeded NASA's funding share, meaning SpaceX invested its own capital to build Dragon 2). NASA provided technical expertise, test facilities, and experienced insight (lessons from Shuttle, etc.), essentially *partnering* rather than purely contracting. The results became apparent in May 2020, when SpaceX's Crew Dragon carried astronauts to the ISS—the first crewed orbital flight by a private company. Boeing's Starliner, while delayed by testing setbacks, was expected to enter service as well. As of June 2025, however, it is unclear when Starliner's next test flight will be, let alone a crewed mission. From NASA's perspective, having **two independent providers** increases redundancy and innovation, a stark contrast to the sole-source Shuttle era. It also introduces market forces: SpaceX and Boeing know that NASA can allocate missions based on performance, so they are incentivized to control costs and maintain schedules. This was exactly what NASA envisioned: *"NASA encourages companies to build their own rockets and spacecraft... and then operates more as a customer, buying back the services,"* rather than owning the systems. The **Time** magazine noted that in theory this should be *"less expensive for NASA and turbocharge the aerospace industry"* by giving companies vehicles that they can also sell to other customers.

Public statements by NASA and industry leaders during this period underscore the new mindset. NASA Administrator Charlie Bolden, at the 2014 crew contract announcement, called it *"the best choice for NASA and the nation"* to go with commercial partners. He and others often cited cost-benefit: NASA analysis suggested that partnering with SpaceX and Orbital for cargo saved 20–30 percent or more compared to in-house development. On the industry side, Boeing's John Elbon highlighted the pride in continuing Boeing's legacy in all human spaceflight programs and promised CST-100 would be *"the most cost-effective, safe and innovative solution"* (a vehicle that would return from its first test flight uncrewed due to multiple thruster failure issues) for U.S. crew access. SpaceX's CEO Elon Musk frequently credited NASA for supporting SpaceX's growth—tweeting in 2021 a simple "**NASA Rules!!**" when SpaceX won the lunar lander contract. Musk also stated in an interview, "*We couldn't have gotten where we are today without the help of NASA... It's an honor to work with them*," reflecting the mutual respect in the partnership. Perhaps most telling was NASA Administrator Jim Bridenstine's remark in 2020 that "*the cost-saving success of Commercial Crew is based on NASA establishing high-level requirements and letting private companies innovate.*" He pointed out that NASA would do similarly for the Artemis Moon lander: set a price per unit (cost per ton to the Moon) and let companies propose solutions. This encapsulates the shift—NASA moves from specifying the **how** to specifying the **what**, and industry takes on more design and financial responsibility. As of June 2025, there is great uncertainty in all of this, as reports indicate that the administration may specifically target SpaceX for punitive contract termination as a result of recent remarks by Elon Musk. This would be illegal but that is where we are in 2025.

By the end of the 2010s, NASA's commercial partnership model had proven itself with cargo and was on the cusp of full success with crew. These programs not only fulfilled NASA's needs (sustaining the ISS, carrying astronauts) but also **seeded a competitive U.S. commercial space sector**. SpaceX, for instance, leveraged NASA contracts to become a major launch provider globally, and new start-ups were inspired by its success. As NASA's 2024 report on commercial space notes, the post-Shuttle era saw "a dramatic rise" in capabilities, with numerous mechanisms (contracts, partnerships, tech transfer, etc.) deployed to nurture commercial growth. NASA had transformed from being just a spacefarer to also being an **enabler of a market**—a role very much aligned with broader political support for private enterprise.

Artemis and Beyond—A New Era of Public–Private Collaboration (2020s)

As NASA entered the 2020s, its partnerships with industry took on even greater significance in the context of the **Artemis program** and the goal of returning humans to the Moon (and eventually Mars). Artemis represents a blend of old and new contracting models. On one hand, NASA's development of the **Space Launch System (SLS)** rocket and **Orion** spacecraft has followed the traditional path of cost-plus contracts with established aerospace giants (Boeing for the SLS core stage, Northrop Grumman for solid boosters, Aerojet Rocketdyne for engines, Lockheed Martin for Orion, etc.). These elements, many of which trace lineage to the canceled Constellation program, encountered cost growth and delays—drawing criticism and prompting Government Accountability Office (GAO) reports calling for better cost transparency. On the other hand, for the lunar landing and surface operations, NASA made a conscious pivot to commercial-style partnerships. The agency chose to procure a **Human Landing System (HLS)** via competition among private companies and to purchase lunar lander services rather than design its own lander from scratch. This approach culminated in 2021 when NASA selected **SpaceX** to develop the first Artemis crewed lander—a modified Starship vehicle—under a **$2.89 billion fixed-price contract.**[10]

This HLS award was historic. It marked the first time a human-rated lunar spacecraft would be developed by a commercial company under a service contract. NASA's selection of SpaceX (over bids from Blue Origin and Dynetics) leveraged SpaceX's willingness to invest its own funds and its rapid innovation culture. The contract is milestone-based: SpaceX only earns the full payment by achieving specific development and flight test objectives, including an uncrewed lunar landing and then the crewed landing for Artemis III. Lisa Watson-Morgan, NASA's HLS program manager, highlighted the **"collaborative approach in working with industry while leveraging NASA's expertise,"** comparing it to Apollo but noting the aim is to do it sustainably and cost-effectively this time. She emphasized that NASA's technical standards and human spaceflight experience are being combined with industry's creativity and speed to achieve the Moon landings. Indeed, NASA experts have been closely embedded with SpaceX during HLS design, much as they were in COTS and Commercial Crew—advising, sharing lessons, but not dictating every solution. This shows the maturation of the partnership model: **shared responsibility**, with NASA ensuring safety and mission assurance, and the company optimizing design and execution. In a concerning move, Lisa Watson-Morgan retired from NASA in June 2025.

Beyond the first landing, NASA quickly signaled it would not make HLS a one-off. The agency announced plans for a follow-on Lander competition (eventually dubbed "Sustainable HLS") to encourage multiple providers for recurring Artemis missions. In 2022, NASA indeed exercised an option with SpaceX for a second crewed landing (Artemis IV) and concurrently initiated a competition (won by a Blue Origin-led team in 2023) for an alternative lander. This multipronged strategy echoes the Commercial Crew dual-provider approach, aiming for redundancy and price discovery. It also reflects political realities—spreading contracts among companies to keep congressional support, reminiscent of earlier eras but now framed as ensuring a competitive marketplace.

Artemis's commercial ethos extends to other lunar systems as well. **Commercial Lunar Payload Services (CLPS)**, started in 2018, is a program where NASA issues "task orders" (essentially requests for commercial performance) for delivering scientific instruments to the Moon's surface via small landers built by private companies. To date, NASA has contracted with a number of start-ups (Intuitive Machines, Astrobotic, etc.) on fixed-price deals to land payloads for a few tens of millions each—an unheard-of low cost for lunar missions. This is another direct outcome of the new partnership mindset: NASA is essentially **outsourcing the entire mission execution to companies**, simply paying for the data or service. As of mid-2025, the first of these commercial lunar landers are poised to attempt landings, opening a new chapter in lunar exploration conducted by commercial lander contractors with NASA as one customer among others. NASA's December 2024 report highlighted CLPS alongside other initiatives like **commercial LEO destinations** (NASA's program to stimulate private space station modules or free-flyers to eventually replace ISS), **commercial development of NASA's next-generation spacesuits** (NASA awarded contracts in 2022 to Axiom Space and Collins Aerospace to develop and supply spacesuit services for ISS and Moonwalks), and even concepts like lunar surface power or mobility provided by industry. Each of these follows the general principle: NASA sets an objective and offers to buy a service or capability, and companies invest and compete to provide it.

The U.S. policy environment in the 2020s has continued to encourage these public–private models. Space exploration remains a national priority with bipartisan backing, but there is also consensus that engaging in the commercial sector can reduce costs and spur innovation. For example, Space Policy Directive-1 (2017), which refocused NASA on the Moon, explicitly called for using commercial partnerships. Congress, while sometimes protective of traditional programs (like SLS), has largely funded the commercial programs as well, seeing the benefits. Notably, the Artemis Accords and international partnerships still rely on NASA's leadership, but NASA leverages industry to fulfill its commitments (for instance, offering partners flights on commercially developed U.S. spacecraft). A business-oriented view would note that NASA's procurement strategy has shifted risk in part to the private sector—companies now invest their own capital and stand to gain commercially if they succeed (and conversely, can lose if they fail, as seen with some CLPS providers encountering setbacks). This arrangement aligns incentives and has attracted venture capital and private investment into space companies at unprecedented levels, multiplying the impact of NASA's dollars.

Landmark Contracts and Outcomes in Artemis

A few contracts deserve "landmark" status in this era. The 2019 award of the SLS Stages contract extension to Boeing (a cost-plus contract that has grown to over $10 billion)[11] drew attention for representing the old model, with critics arguing that it lacked cost control. In contrast, the 2021 HLS award to SpaceX for $2.9 billion was landmark for its bold fixed-price nature and for entrusting a historically unprecedented task (human lunar landing) to a single commercial player. Another is the 2021 contracts under the Commercial LEO Destinations (CLD) project, where NASA granted ~$400 million combined to four companies (including Blue Origin, Northrop Grumman, Nanoracks, and Axiom Space) to design private space stations.[12] While much smaller than Apollo-era contracts, these CLD agreements are seed investments similar to COTS, aiming to ensure a seamless transition from the government-owned ISS to privately owned stations by the end of the decade.

Industry leaders have spoken about these partnerships in business terms. Gwynne Shotwell, President of SpaceX, has praised NASA for being a "smart customer" and incubator, noting that NASA's early contracts gave SpaceX credibility to win other business. Blue Origin's leadership, although initially critical of the sole-source HLS award, pivoted to collaborating on the second lander and lauded NASA's commitment to sustained lunar presence via commercial means. Traditional contractors such as Lockheed Martin and Boeing have also adapted: Lockheed now markets its Orion capsule for potential commercial use (e.g., around the Moon tourism or deep space habitat modules), and Boeing formed a start-up-style subsidiary to pursue a commercial space station (the Orbital Reef project with Blue Origin). These moves indicate that even legacy firms recognize that the industry is shifting from pure cost-plus contracting to a mix of government and commercial customers, often requiring co-investment.

In summary, the early 2020s solidify a **hybrid partnership model** at NASA. For certain critical systems with no immediate commercial market (like heavy-lift rockets capable of beyond-LEO crew missions), NASA continues to fund development in a traditional way. But for a wide range of other needs—launch services, crew transport, lunar landers, surface operations, and space station modules—NASA is harnessing the power of the marketplace. The agency has become **one customer among many** (e.g., SpaceX's Starship may serve NASA for HLS, but SpaceX also intends it for its own Mars plans and commercial launches), which in theory drives down NASA's costs long term. As NASA stated in its 2024 analysis, "*the agency's use of commercial capabilities has progressed from being the exception to the default method for many missions,*" and the level of technical development in this post-Shuttle commercial era is comparable to the Apollo era's space race. That is a remarkable transformation in how NASA does business.

Looking ahead, NASA's Artemis ambitions—establishing a sustainable lunar base and preparing for human Mars expeditions—rely on continuing and expanding these public–private collaborations. The U.S. government's space goals are now explicitly tied to fostering a **"space economy"** where private innovation flourishes alongside national objectives. From the 1950s to the 2020s, NASA's engagement with industry has come full circle in some ways: it began with contracting companies to achieve a government goal (Mercury, Apollo), and it now often contracts companies to achieve government goals (ISS supply, Moon landing)—but with the crucial difference that today the companies may own the infrastructure and can repurpose it commercially. This evolution has been shaped by changing political philosophies, budgetary realities, and the maturing of aerospace technology where private actors can sometimes lead.

NASA's collaboration with private industry remains a **cornerstone of its success**, and the partnership continues to be redefined with each generation. As history has shown, when NASA and American industry innovate together, from the Saturn V to the Dragon capsule, the results can astonish the world. The challenges of the future—from Mars landings to commercial space stations—will undoubtedly spawn new partnership models and landmark agreements. Yet the underlying principle endures: NASA's mission to push the frontiers of space is inextricably linked with the capabilities, ingenuity, and enterprise of the private sector. Each era— Apollo, Shuttle, ISS, Commercial Crew, and Artemis—builds on the lessons of before, reinforcing that **the public–private partnership is not a trend but the very fabric of U.S. space exploration**.

Protectionism, Politics, and Pork: Why the History Matters

The extent of NASA's reliance on industry manufacturing, supplying, and managing mission development and operation has changed back and forth over time. Ever since the current NASA center landscape was cemented during the Apollo era, procurement decisions have always had varying amounts of protectionism, politics, and pork. The assignment of projects, the selection of vendors, and even the long-term goals themselves have never been purely outcome-based. A wise NASA contractor considers these factors and looks ahead while developing plans.

Story Time 1: "Nepotism Nepotism Nepotism"

My first position at JPL did not have an auspicious start. It was in the export control office, which is a form of regulatory compliance for international sharing of certain types of information. Not one to ever waste a connection in the pursuit of a job, my initial interview came via my dad's girlfriend's hula dancing teacher's roommate. I am not

(*Continued*)

(*Continued*)

making that up. That person knew the deputy director of JPL and helped me with an introduction. When I got the job, I encountered hostility from the other people in that department, which mystified me. Later it turned out that the manager had misunderstood the nature of my connection and thought that I was the grandson of a deputy director.

I discovered that on my first day she had sent an email to the team announcing me with the text "NEPOTISM NEPOTISM NEPOTISM" in the subject line. This manager was eventually fired for that and other grossly unprofessional conduct, a very high bar to reach at JPL unfortunately. I'm glad things happened that way actually because it showed me what I did not want to do very early on and helped me find the path I am on today.

CHAPTER 2

How It Works Now

Types of Contracts and Funding Mechanisms Used by NASA

NASA employs a variety of contract types and funding instruments to advance its missions. The appropriate mechanism is chosen based on the nature of the work and who the primary beneficiary is. In general, procurement contracts are used when NASA is acquiring goods or services for its own use, whereas grants and cooperative agreements are used as financial assistance to support research or projects that primarily benefit the public or the recipient.

NASA also makes use of other special agreements and funding mechanisms (such as SAAs, Cooperative Research and Development Agreements (CRADAs), Small Business Innovation Research (SBIR) awards, and prize competitions) to partner with industry, academia, and the public. Following is a detailed overview of each type, with key characteristics, purposes, and examples.

Procurement Contracts

Procurement contracts are the standard agreements NASA uses to acquire supplies, services, or research and development for the direct benefit or use of the Agency (the federal government) (Partnering with NASA—NASA). These contracts are legally binding and are governed by the FAR and the NASA FAR Supplement (in the NASA FAR Supplement). Key characteristics include:

Purpose

To buy something for NASA—whether it's hardware, spacecraft, research services, facility construction, and so on. If NASA is the primary beneficiary of the work, a contract is required by law. For example, NASA uses contracts to procure launch services, develop spacecraft, build facilities, and obtain consulting or engineering support.

Key Characteristics

Contracts include detailed specifications, deliverables, and performance requirements, with NASA exercising oversight to ensure the contractor meets its obligations. They are fully enforceable; failure to perform can lead to penalties or termination. Unlike assistance awards, contracts are subject to FAR rules on competition, cost accounting, audits, socioeconomic requirements, and so on. NASA must generally compete for contracts and manage them closely since taxpayer funds are buying a direct NASA need.

Types of Contracts

NASA uses various FAR contract types depending on project risk and requirements (per FAR Part 16). These range from firm-fixed-price (FFP) contracts (where the price is set and the contractor bears cost risk) to cost-reimbursement contracts (where NASA pays allowable costs and often a fee) (Final Report—IG-24-001—NASA's Transition of the Space Launch System to a Commercial Services Contract). For high-risk, complex development (like new spacecraft or rockets), NASA has often used cost-plus contracts (e.g., cost-plus-award-fee)—the government covers the costs and adds an incentive fee based on performance (Final Report—IG-24-001—NASA's Transition of the Space Launch System to a Commercial Services Contract). This shifts most cost risk to the government but is useful when precise requirements or costs are uncertain. In contrast, for well-defined or commercial services, NASA prefers fixed-price contracts to control costs. NASA also uses Indefinite Delivery/Indefinite Quantity contracts and purchase orders for recurring or smaller needs (NASA Procurement Data View—Help).

Examples

Most large NASA projects are executed via procurement contracts. For instance, NASA's contract with Boeing to build the SLS rocket core stage is a cost-plus-award-fee contract, meaning Boeing is reimbursed for costs and can earn award fees based on NASA's evaluation of performance (Final Report—IG-24-001—NASA's Transition of the Space Launch System to a Commercial Services Contract). On the other hand, NASA's CRS contracts with SpaceX and Northrop Grumman to deliver cargo to the ISS are fixed-price service contracts—NASA pays a set price per mission, putting the onus on the companies to manage costs efficiently (Final Report—IG-24-001—NASA's Transition of the Space Launch System to a Commercial Services Contract). NASA has likewise awarded fixed-price contracts to companies like SpaceX, Boeing, and Axiom for services such as crew transport and astronaut spacesuits (Final Report—IG-24-001—NASA's Transition of the Space Launch System to a Commercial Services Contract). All these ensure that NASA obtains the goods or services it needs under enforceable terms.

Grants (Financial Assistance)

Grants are a form of financial assistance NASA provides to external organizations (universities, research institutions, companies, state governments, etc.) to support a public purpose or stimulate research, rather than to acquire something for NASA's direct use. In a grant, NASA is essentially funding the recipient's project for their benefit (and the broader public benefit), with minimal agency involvement in the work. Key points about grants:

Purpose

Used when the aim is to support or stimulate scientific research, technology development, education, or other activities that benefit the public, as opposed to meeting a specific NASA mission procurement need). For example, NASA issues many grants to academic researchers studying Earth science, astronomy, aeronautics, and so on, and to STEM education programs. These projects advance knowledge or public goals aligned with NASA's interests, but they are not deliverables that NASA directly uses.

Key Characteristics

Grants are governed by financial assistance regulations (Title 2 of the Code of Federal Regulations) rather than the FAR. The recipient has a high degree of autonomy in carrying out the project; NASA does not exercise day-to-day control or direction. Importantly, NASA provides funding but generally does not provide substantial personnel involvement—that is, no "hands-on" collaboration by NASA in the work (that would make it a cooperative agreement). NASA's role is mainly to oversee compliance with grant terms and ensure that the money is used for the intended purpose, but not to manage the project's details. Grants do not stipulate deliverables for NASA and usually do not result in NASA-owned property or services for the Agency. They also typically forbid any fee or profit; they only reimburse allowable project costs.

Administration

NASA's grants follow standard federal grant practices (per the Federal Grant and Cooperative Agreement Act and Uniform Guidance). They require proposals (often via NASA Research Announcements or solicitations on grants.gov) and are awarded by a grant officer. Monitoring involves progress reports and financial reports, but less rigor than a contract. The NASA Shared Services Center manages many grant awards for the agency (Grants Policy and Compliance Team—NASA).

Examples

NASA invests heavily in grants for research and education. For instance, NASA spends over $1.1 billion per year on grants and cooperative agreements across its mission directorates.[13] Typical grants include research awards to university scientists (e.g., a grant to analyze data from a NASA telescope or to develop new materials for aerospace), NASA's Space Grant program awards to universities for STEM student training, and grants to museums or nonprofits for public outreach. Under the annual ROSES (Research Opportunities in Space and Earth Sciences) solicitations, NASA selects dozens of proposals for scientific research grants. In these cases, the funded researchers carry out the studies and publish results, thereby contributing to NASA's broader mission and public knowledge, but NASA is not "buying" a product—it is supporting the research. The distinction is codified by law: if the direct beneficiary of the work is the public (through new knowledge or capabilities) rather than NASA itself, a grant or cooperative agreement is the appropriate instrument.

Cooperative Agreements
(Financial Assistance With Collaboration)

A cooperative agreement is another type of financial assistance instrument, very similar to a grant in purpose (supporting a public-purpose project), except that it involves "substantial involvement" by NASA in the activity. In other words, NASA and the recipient collaborate on the project in some meaningful way. Key aspects of cooperative agreements:

Purpose

Like grants, cooperative agreements are used to fund projects that benefit the public or the recipient, not to acquire goods for NASA. The projects can be R&D, technology demonstrations, education initiatives, and so on. The difference is that NASA intends to participate actively in the project alongside the award recipient. This substantial NASA involvement is planned *from the outset* due to the project's needs.

NASA's Substantial Involvement

What qualifies as "substantial involvement" can vary, but it generally means that NASA is contributing resources, expertise, or personnel to the effort in a collaborative manner. For example, NASA might provide laboratory facilities, equipment, or testing services, or NASA scientists might work jointly with the recipient's researchers on the project. NASA could also be involved in project decision-making (e.g., approving stages of work or helping modify the objectives) as a partner. Importantly, NASA's involvement is to support the recipient's success, not to direct the work for NASA's own deliverables. (Cooperative agreements are still not used for NASA to obtain its own deliverables; if NASA needed a deliverable, it would use a contract.) Other than the cooperative aspect, the legal framework is the same as grants—they fall under the same 2 CFR assistance rules, with no fee, and are handled by grant/cooperative agreement officers rather than contracting officers.

When Used

NASA chooses a cooperative agreement instead of a grant when both parties will benefit from working together and duplication of effort can be avoided (NASA Procurement Data View—Help). For instance, if a university and a NASA center are both researching a similar technology, a cooperative agreement allows them to pool resources and expertise, resulting in a better outcome for the public and NASA's mission interest. NASA policy notes that coops are typically used "to accomplish a mutually desired goal for a current NASA project where both parties have done some preliminary work which, if continued separately, would result in unnecessary duplication of costs." (NASA Procurement Data View—Help).

Examples

Many NASA partnerships with universities or nonprofits are structured as cooperative agreements. One notable example is the agreement with the Center for the Advancement of Science in Space (CASIS) to manage the ISS U.S. National Laboratory. In 2011, NASA awarded a $136 million cooperative agreement to CASIS to run the ISS National Lab,[14] with NASA and CASIS working together to facilitate research by other organizations in microgravity (A Strategy for the Future of the International Space Station National Laboratory (ISSNL) and Commercial LEO Development). (NASA provides the ISS platform and expertise, and CASIS manages outreach and research selection, which is a collaborative arrangement.) NASA has also used cooperative agreements to establish research institutes (e.g., joint research centers where a university leads and NASA researchers collaborate on space technology development), and to partner with industry or state organizations on technology demonstrations. Essentially, whenever NASA wants to not only fund an external project but also actively contribute to it, a cooperative agreement is the tool. Aside from CASIS, another example is NASA's partnerships through Cooperative Agreement Notices for advanced space technology projects, where NASA centers team with companies or academia, each contributing personnel or resources to achieve a technology milestone. The Space Technology Research Institutes funded by NASA are cooperative agreements that bring together university consortia and NASA experts to tackle cutting-edge research areas.

Space Act Agreements (Other Transactions)

SAAs are unique contracting mechanisms available only to NASA, authorized under the National Aeronautics and Space Act.[15] They are sometimes referred to as NASA's form of "Other Transaction Authority (OTA)." SAAs are *not* procurement contracts or standard grants; instead, they are flexible partnership agreements that allow NASA to work with a wide range of partners (industry, academia, other governments, even international entities) to advance NASA's mission in situations where a contract, grant, or cooperative agreement is not suitable. Key points about SAAs:

Legal Basis and Purpose

The Space Act (51 U.S.C. §20113) gives NASA broad authority to "enter into and perform contracts, leases, cooperative agreements, or other transactions as may be necessary in the conduct of its work" (Space Act Agreement—Wikipedia). SAAs fall under the "other transactions" part of this authority. They are generally used to form partnerships or collaborations that fulfill NASA's mission objectives in innovative ways. Crucially, NASA can use an SAA in cases where the goal cannot be met through a standard contract or assistance award. This might be because the relationship is truly collaborative or because the partner won't agree to FAR contract terms, and so on. SAAs give NASA more flexibility in terms and conditions than FAR contracts do (e.g., they are not bound by all federal procurement regulations. This flexibility can attract commercial partners who might shy away from traditional government contracts.

Types of Space Act Agreements

NASA defines several subtypes of SAA:

Reimbursable SAA

NASA performs work for a partner or shares a NASA capability, and the partner reimburses NASA's costs (Partnering with NASA—NASA). For instance, a company might pay NASA to use a wind tunnel or to test a component at a NASA facility. NASA enters these when it has unique facilities or expertise that others need, and it can offer them without hindering its own missions.

Nonreimbursable SAA

A collaborative partnership with no exchange of funds (Partnering with NASA). Both NASA and the partner contribute resources (e.g., labor, equipment, facilities) to a shared objective, each covering their own expenses. This is often used when NASA and, say, a company or university want to work together on a research project or technology demo for mutual benefit, but neither is paying the other. Each side does what it does best, and they share the results.

Funded SAA

NASA provides funding to an external partner (much like a grant) to accomplish a goal for NASA's mission, when NASA cannot achieve that goal via a procurement contract or standard grant/cooperative agreement. A funded SAA is somewhat similar to a cooperative agreement, but it falls under the Space Act authority. By policy, funded SAAs are used rarely and require competition. They essentially allow NASA to fund the industry directly to develop capabilities that NASA needs without the full FAR contracting process.

International SAA

Either reimbursable or nonreimbursable, but with a foreign entity as the partner (Space Act Agreement—Wikipedia). NASA frequently uses SAAs to collaborate with foreign space agencies or companies on projects of mutual interest, since SAAs can accommodate unique legal arrangements and no-exchange-of-funds deals with international partners. (These often require State Department coordination as well.)

Key Characteristics

SAAs are flexible and customizable. NASA and the partner negotiate the terms, including milestones, intellectual property rights, resource sharing, and termination conditions, without being strictly bound by FAR clauses. They are not considered procurement instruments, so they are not used to directly purchase goods/services for NASA, and they typically do not involve the standard contract oversight or contract enforcement mechanisms. Instead, they are structured around milestones and mutual interest. If it's a funded SAA, NASA may pay upon completion of specified milestones (which is different from a cost-reimbursement contract; if milestones aren't met, NASA may not pay). Accountability in SAAs comes from the agreement terms and the fact that both parties want the project to succeed, rather than from the government imposing penalties.

Notable Examples

SAAs have been instrumental in some of NASA's biggest recent programs. For example, under the COTS program in the mid-2000s, NASA funded SAAs to partner with SpaceX and Orbital Sciences (now Northrop Grumman) to develop commercial cargo spacecraft for the ISS. These agreements provided NASA funding in increments when the companies met development milestones, and in return, the companies developed rockets and capsules that NASA could later use. Unlike traditional contracts, the companies retained more ownership of the design and could commercialize the services.

This Approach Succeeded

SpaceX's Falcon 9 rocket and Dragon cargo capsule were developed under a funded SAA, leading to operational resupply missions. Similarly, NASA's CCDev program started with SAAs—NASA linked SAAs with companies such as SpaceX, Boeing, Blue Origin, and Sierra Nevada to develop crew transportation capabilities (Space Act Agreement—Wikipedia). These were competitively awarded, milestone-based agreements that jump-started the crew capsules (SpaceX's Crew Dragon, Boeing's Starliner). Once those systems were developed, NASA moved to traditional fixed-price contracts for actual crew flight services. In addition to these funded SAAs, NASA extensively uses nonreimbursable SAAs—for example, collaborating with companies on advanced aeronautics research where each side shares test data, or partnering with organizations on STEM education initiatives. Internationally, agreements with other space agencies for projects like the Artemis program (e.g., Canada contributing a robotic arm, Europe contributing a service module) are often structured as no-funds-exchanged SAAs. Overall, SAAs are NASA's primary vehicle for partnerships outside the standard contract/grant framework (Partnering with NASA—NASA (SAA, SAA, SAA), giving the Agency a flexible way to engage the private sector and international partners in achieving NASA's goals.

Cooperative Research and Development Agreements (CRADAs)

A CRADA is another partnership mechanism, commonly used by federal laboratories under the Government's technology transfer laws. A CRADA is defined as a formal agreement between one or more federal laboratories and one or more nonfederal parties to collaborate in R&D. NASA, as a federal science agency, has the authority to enter CRADAs (under the Federal Technology Transfer Act, 15 U.S.C. §3710a) to work with outside entities on research and development. Key points include:

Nature of CRADAs

Under a CRADA, NASA (through one of its research centers or labs) and a partner (e.g., a company, university, or other entity) jointly work on a research or technology project. NASA can provide personnel, facilities, equipment, expertise, and other resources for collaboration

(CRADAs—Cooperative Research and Development Agreements | U.S. Department of the Interior). The partner can provide resources and even funds to NASA, but importantly, NASA cannot provide funding to the partner under a CRADA (CRADAs—Cooperative Research and Development Agreements | U.S. Department of the Interior). In other words, no direct exchange of federal funds to the nonfederal party is allowed. This distinguishes CRADAs from funded SAAs or grants—a CRADA is about sharing *effort and resources* rather than NASA granting money. Both parties typically sign a Joint Work Statement outlining their contributions and the project scope. CRADAs are intended to leverage federal lab capabilities to assist industry or academia in developing new technology that aligns with the lab's mission.

Purpose

The primary purpose is technology transfer and collaboration. CRADAs allow NASA centers to partner with external innovators to push a technology forward, while ensuring that both sides can share in the resulting know-how. Often, the external partner gains access to NASA's unique facilities or expertise, and NASA benefits by advancing its research objectives or gaining data. CRADAs support NASA's mandate to disseminate and commercialize technology for the nation's benefit. They are commonly used for early-stage R&D, testing, or prototyping efforts.

Key Characteristics

CRADAs are quite flexible agreements (not subject to FAR or typical procurement rules). They usually include terms on how intellectual property is handled—for example, the partner might get the option to license any inventions that result. Because no funds are paid out by NASA, the agreement focuses on who contributes, what resources are used, and how the results will be shared. CRADAs are typically no-cost to NASA aside from in-kind contributions, so they're easier to approve in some cases. They can be faster to establish than contracts, and they provide a mechanism for industry to work with NASA labs without going through a procurement process. In essence, a CRADA is similar to a nonreimbursable SAA in that both sides work together and each bears its own costs. (In fact, NASA often uses the term "partnership agreements" mainly in reference to SAAs, which are "similar to CRADAs" used at other agencies.

NASA's Use

While NASA's primary partnership tool with industry is the SAA, it also uses CRADAs, particularly in areas of pure research or when collaborating through its field centers. For instance, a NASA research center like Ames or Glenn might enter a CRADA with an aerospace company to jointly investigate a new propulsion material—NASA provides its lab and engineers, the company provides sample materials and funding for testing, and both share technical data. The NASA Inspector General and Advisory Council have at times encouraged NASA to expand the use of CRADAs to engage commercial partners where appropriate. CRADAs are a standard instrument across government labs (e.g., Department of Defense labs and Department of Energy labs use them heavily); at NASA, they complement SAAs as part of the Agency's toolkit for R&D partnerships.

Examples

Many CRADAs at NASA are not publicized as widely as major contracts, but they cover a range of projects. For example, NASA's Kennedy Space Center has used CRADAs to partner with companies on advanced propellants and lunar landing technologies. NASA's aeronautics researchers have entered CRADAs with aviation companies to test aircraft concepts using NASA wind tunnels or simulation facilities. In one notable case outside NASA, a CRADA between the U.S. Air Force and SpaceX was used to cooperatively develop and test a new range safety system for rockets, illustrating how government and industry can team up under CRADAs. For NASA specifically, if a technology is promising but not yet tied to a procurement program, a CRADA can facilitate joint exploration of that tech. It's one of the "nonprocurement vehicles" (along with grants, cooperative agreements, and SAAs) that NASA can use to engage partners in R&D.

Small Business Innovation Research (SBIR/STTR) Contracts

NASA participates in the federal SBIR and Small Business Technology Transfer (STTR) programs, which are special funding mechanisms aimed at stimulating technological innovation in the small business sector. While these are government-wide programs, NASA's implementation is worth noting. SBIR and STTR awards are usually structured as procurement contracts (sometimes called SBIR contracts), but they function as seed funding for R&D projects by small companies, rather than traditional large-scale procurement. Key features include:

Program Structure

NASA SBIR/STTR awards are given in phases. Phase I awards are small, short-term contracts (for feasibility studies of a new idea). At NASA, a typical SBIR Phase I contract runs six months with up to $125,000 in funding (Small Business Innovation Research (SBIR) and Small Business Technology Transfer (STTR)—NASA). If Phase I is successful, the company can compete for Phase II, which provides a larger contract to develop the prototype or technology—NASA's SBIR Phase II contracts last up to 24 months with up to $750,000 in funding (Small Business Innovation Research (SBIR) and Small Business Technology Transfer (STTR)—NASA). There are sometimes Phase III or follow-on opportunities (not funded by the SBIR program itself—often Phase III means the technology gets a procurement contract or third-party investment to transition it to application).[16] STTR is a sister program to SBIR that requires small businesses to partner with a research institution (like a university). NASA's STTR Phase I and II contract amounts are similar to SBIR.

Purpose

The purpose of SBIR/STTR is to encourage small businesses to develop innovative technologies that NASA could use. It's a way for NASA to tap into the creativity of start-ups and small firms, and potentially benefit from those new technologies in its missions. In return, the small businesses get funding and a chance to commercialize their innovations. The work is often aligned with NASA's needs (the Agency releases specific R&D topics each year seeking solutions via SBIR proposals).

Characteristics

SBIR/STTR awards at NASA are contracts, so they are governed by applicable procurement rules, but they are simplified and tailored for R&D. These contracts are usually fixed-price or FFP to cover the scope of work defined in the proposal. They have milestones/deliverables (e.g., a report or prototype at the end of Phase I). However, unlike large FAR contracts, SBIR contracts use streamlined terms, and the process is designed to be small-business-friendly. There is a statutory set-aside of NASA's R&D budget for SBIR/STTR, ensuring funding each year. Notably, SBIR/STTR contracts allow small businesses to retain intellectual property rights to their inventions, while giving the government a license to use them—this helps companies commercialize the tech in wider markets.

Examples

Every year, NASA awards hundreds of SBIR contracts across many technical areas (aeronautics, propulsion, robotics, materials, etc.). For example, a small firm might win a Phase I SBIR contract to develop a new sensor for spacecraft. If successful, they may receive a Phase II contract to build and test a prototype sensor. Many technologies currently used by NASA started as SBIR projects. One success story is the company Made In Space, which received SBIR funding in its early days to develop 3D printing for microgravity, eventually leading to a 3D printer being used on the ISS.[17] Another example is Paragon Space Development, which won SBIR contracts for life support system components, some of which fed into designs for Artemis life support. While individually small (hundreds of thousands of dollars), SBIR contracts collectively represent a significant funding mechanism and an important avenue for small businesses to work with NASA. In summary, SBIR/STTR contracts are a procurement mechanism tailored to R&D innovation, bridging the gap between pure research and larger scale NASA acquisition programs.

Prize Competitions and Challenges

In addition to formal contracts and agreements, NASA also uses prize competitions as a funding mechanism to spur innovation. Under programs like NASA's Centennial Challenges (part of the Prizes and Challenges program), the Agency offers monetary prizes to individuals or teams that can achieve specific technical goals or solve particular problems. Prizes are authorized by Congress (e.g., via the Space Act and federal prize authority laws) and have become a popular tool to engage the public and private sectors in NASA's mission.

Key Points

How Prizes Work: NASA publicly announces a challenge goal—for example, "build a lunar rover that can drill for ice" or "design a new astronaut glove"—along with rules and a prize purse. Teams independently work on the challenge, without NASA funding them upfront. The prize money is awarded only to the winner(s) who meet the challenge criteria first or best. This model is sometimes called an "inducement prize contest": it induces innovation by dangling a reward. It's essentially pay-for-performance—if no one achieves the goal, NASA doesn't pay the prize. This approach can be very cost-effective, as it leverages competitors' own resources and creativity.

Purpose

NASA uses prize challenges to crowdsource solutions and encourage breakthroughs in areas of interest. Prizes attract not just traditional contractors but also inventors, small companies, academia, and citizen problem-solvers who might not engage through normal contracts (Prizes, Challenges, and Crowdsourcing). They help NASA get fresh ideas and advance technology without bearing all the development costs. Prizes are particularly useful for problems where NASA is unsure of the best approach and is open to a variety of solutions. They also create public enthusiasm by making NASA's problems into competitions that teams can rally around.

Key Characteristics

Prize competitions are open competitions—typically, anyone who meets the eligibility criteria (often U.S. citizens or entities for NASA prizes) can compete. NASA usually partners with nonprofit organizations to administer the challenges and verify results. The prize amounts can range widely, from a few thousand dollars to millions, depending on the difficulty. The rules are published in challenge documents, and there is often a fixed timeframe to achieve the goal. Because these are not contracts, the competitors are not NASA contractors; they're voluntary participants, and NASA doesn't direct their work. However, NASA may provide some support, such as challenge-related information or test opportunities. The legal instrument for a prize is usually a simplified agreement or registration, not a procurement contract—the funding is given as an award to the winner, categorized under NASA's prize authority. An advantage of this mechanism is that NASA only pays for success, as noted, and it can stimulate the development of technologies that later NASA or others can use.

Examples

NASA's Centennial Challenges program has run numerous high-profile contests. For instance, the Sample Return Robot Challenge offered prizes for autonomous robots that could navigate and collect samples; the winning team received $750,000 after demonstrating the required tasks.[18] The Astronaut Glove Challenge gave awards (hundreds of thousands of dollars) to improved spacesuit glove designs. The Lunar Lander Challenge, cosponsored by NASA, awarded $2 million in prizes to Masten Space Systems and Armadillo Aerospace for successful free-flying rocket lander tests. More recently, NASA has offered the 3D-Printed Habitat Challenge (multimillion dollar prizes for 3D-printed housing concepts for Mars) and the CO_2 Conversion Challenge to turn carbon dioxide into useful compounds.

As of 2023, NASA announced the Luna# Recycle Challenge with a $3 million prize purse for technologies to recycle polymer waste on long-duration lunar missions. This is an example of how prize competitions target cutting-edge problems—multiple teams are likely working on creative recycling solutions right now, and only the best will claim the prize. In addition, NASA engages the public through smaller challenges (including coding challenges on platforms like TopCoder and student challenges) to broaden participation in its innovation efforts. Prizes and challenges have become an integral part of NASA's R&D strategy, complementing traditional contracts and grants by reaching a different audience and paying only for outcomes.

NASA's funding and contracting landscape is diverse, tailored to different needs. Procurement contracts (ranging from small purchase orders to multibillion-dollar development contracts) remain the primary means to acquire mission-critical hardware, services, and technology for NASA's own use. Grants and cooperative agreements enable NASA to support the broader scientific community and foster innovation and education, with cooperative agreements adding the benefit of direct collaboration. Through SAAs and CRADAs, NASA forges partnerships that leverage external capabilities and share resources in ways standard contracts can't, accelerating progress in research and commercial space development. Specialized programs like SBIR/STTR bridge the gap for small businesses to contribute technology via phased contracts, and prize competitions invite the ingenuity of the masses to solve NASA's toughest challenges with reward-based incentives. Each of these contract types and funding mechanisms has distinct characteristics and rules, but all serve to advance NASA's mission of exploration, scientific discovery, and aeronautical research. By using the right instrument for the right situation, NASA can engage with virtually any entity—be it a large aerospace prime contractor, a university lab, a start-up company, or a garage inventor—and harness their contributions to further humanity's reach into space and knowledge. The variety of NASA's contracting mechanisms exemplifies the Agency's flexible approach to problem-solving and collaboration, ensuring that mission objectives are met in the most effective way possible.

Contract Disputes

Where we find contracts, we find lawsuits. Here are a few examples.

NASA Contract Dispute Lawsuits Since 2000

NASA's large contracts often face disputes from companies that lose out or encounter problems during performance. Many of these disputes since 2000 have involved procurement protests (often filed with the GAO) and occasional lawsuits in federal courts. The following sections are summaries of major cases, focusing on procurement disagreements, contractor performance issues, legal arguments, and outcomes, with sources for further reading.

Artemis Human Landing System Contract— Blue Origin Versus NASA (2021)

Parties and Context

In 2021, NASA awarded a single contract for its Artemis HLS—the lunar lander to return humans to the Moon—to SpaceX. Blue Origin (led by Jeff Bezos) and Dynetics (a Leidos company), both losing bidders, protested this decision. Blue Origin subsequently filed a lawsuit against NASA in the U.S. Court of Federal Claims, with SpaceX joining as an intervenor.

Nature of the Dispute

The solicitation initially suggested that NASA might select multiple companies to develop lunar landers. Blue Origin argued that NASA improperly chose only one winner due to budget constraints without giving others a chance to adjust their proposals. They claimed that NASA unfairly waived a requirement for SpaceX and conducted unequal evaluations. Essentially, Blue Origin alleged that the selection process was arbitrary, capricious, and violated procurement law.

Legal Arguments

In the GAO protest, Blue Origin and Dynetics contended that NASA should have made more than one award or at least amended the solicitation when funding became an issue. They also argued that NASA's evaluation, favoring SpaceX, was flawed and that SpaceX got special treatment (waiver of a flight readiness requirement). NASA countered that the announcement allowed a single award based on available funding, and SpaceX's proposal was the highest rated and lowest cost, making it the clear best value.

Outcome

GAO denied the protests in July 2021,[19] finding NASA did not violate procurement law by selecting only one contractor. GAO concluded that NASA's decision to make one award due to insufficient funding was permissible and that the evaluations were reasonable. Although GAO noted a minor requirement was waived for SpaceX, it ruled this caused no meaningful prejudice to the other bidders. Blue Origin then pursued its case in court, but in November 2021, the Court of Federal Claims dismissed Blue Origin's lawsuit. The judge agreed that Blue Origin lacked standing because its bid was significantly higher-priced and noncompliant, and additionally found NASA's award was not arbitrary or capricious. This allowed NASA and SpaceX to proceed with the $2.9 billion HLS contract.

Commercial Crew Program Contract— Sierra Nevada Versus NASA (2014–2015)

Parties and Context

In September 2014, NASA awarded its CCtCap contracts to SpaceX and Boeing to develop vehicles to ferry astronauts to the ISS. Sierra Nevada Corporation's proposal (the *Dream Chaser* spaceplane) was not selected. Sierra Nevada filed a GAO protest on September 26, 2014, to challenge the awards.[20] As required by law, NASA initially issued a stop-work order to SpaceX and Boeing pending the GAO decision. However, on October 9, NASA lifted the stop-work order citing schedule risks to the ISS if work was delayed.

Nature of the Dispute

Sierra Nevada's protest argued that NASA's evaluation was flawed and that *Dream Chaser* offered a safe, cost-effective alternative that NASA unfairly disregarded. When NASA overrode the stop-work freeze, Sierra

Nevada viewed it as improper. On October 15, 2014, Sierra Nevada filed suit in the Court of Federal Claims seeking a temporary restraining order to reinstate the stop-work halt on Boeing and SpaceX's contracts while the GAO protest was ongoing.

Legal Arguments

Sierra Nevada asserted that NASA's decision to resume contract performance before GAO's verdict was "arbitrary and capricious" and an abuse of discretion. The company argued that NASA hadn't shown that overriding the stay was justified by urgent circumstances, and that continuing work would prejudice its chances of a fair reconsideration. NASA, on the other hand, argued that delays in the Commercial Crew Program would pose risks to ISS operations and crew safety, justifying the need to press forward.

Outcome

The federal court denied Sierra Nevada's attempt to reinstate the stop-work order, allowing NASA's override to stand (the court proceedings on the injunction were largely overtaken by events). Ultimately, on January 5, 2015, GAO denied Sierra Nevada's protest of the contract awards. GAO's decision (under protective order) essentially upheld NASA's selection of SpaceX and Boeing. With the protest denied, NASA proceeded fully with the SpaceX and Boeing contracts. Sierra Nevada did not receive a CCtCap contract, though it later won contracts in a subsequent program to use Dream Chaser for cargo delivery.

ISS Resupply Services Contract— PlanetSpace Versus NASA (2008–2009)

Parties and Context

In late 2008, NASA awarded CRS contracts to SpaceX and Orbital Sciences to deliver cargo to the ISS, in preparation for the Space Shuttle's retirement. A third bidder, PlanetSpace Inc. (PSI)—a team that included Lockheed Martin, Boeing, and Alliant Techsystems (ATK) as partners— lost out on the $3.5 billion deal. In January 2009, PSI filed a protest with GAO, citing 19 separate issues with NASA's decision-making.[21]

Nature of the Dispute

PSI contended that NASA's Source Selection officials unfairly discounted the strengths of its proposal. The company argued that it had major aerospace teammates with excellent past performance, yet NASA focused on PSI own lack of experience and financial concerns. PSI claimed that NASA's source selection authority deviated from the evaluation board's findings in a way that undermined PSI bid (sometimes referring to an alleged "dilution" of favorable findings by a top NASA official).

Legal Arguments

In the GAO protest, PSI legal team argued that NASA misevaluated the proposal by overemphasizing risks and underestimating the contributions of PSI heavyweight subcontractors. They pointed to the strong past performance of Lockheed, Boeing, and ATK as subcontractors and argued that NASA should have given more credit to those strengths. NASA responded that while the partner companies had impressive credentials, PSI itself was a recently formed entity with little relevant experience, and much of the work and risk would have fallen on subcontractors, creating a high-risk setup. NASA also had concerns about PSI financial plan and its heavy reliance on cost-plus subcontracting, which could lead to overruns.

Outcome

GAO denied PSI protest in May 2009, affirming that NASA acted reasonably in its evaluation. GAO's General Counsel Gary Kepplinger noted that NASA reasonably concluded that PSI lack of its own technical/management capability and the high financial risk of its proposal outweighed the favorable past performance of its partners. In other words, NASA was justified in viewing PSI bid as too risky. Following the GAO loss, PSI took the case to the Court of Federal Claims, but the court did not grant PSI the contract either (it ultimately upheld NASA's decision after reviewing additional facets of the procurement). The CRS contracts remained with SpaceX and Orbital, which successfully began cargo flights to the ISS in the ensuing years.

Lucy Mission Launch Contract—
SpaceX Versus NASA (2019)

Parties and Context

In January 2019, NASA awarded ULA a contract to launch the Lucy planetary science probe to the Trojan asteroids, for an announced price of $148.3 million. SpaceX, which had bid for the job, promptly filed a protest with GAO in February 2019.[22] This triggered an automatic stop-work order on ULA's launch contract while the protest was under review.

Nature of the Dispute

SpaceX argued that NASA's award to ULA was unjustifiably expensive. In a public statement, SpaceX noted that it had offered a solution with high confidence of success "at a price dramatically lower" than ULA's, and that paying "vastly more" to ULA was not in the taxpayers' best interest. Essentially, SpaceX claimed that it could launch Lucy on a Falcon 9 rocket much more cheaply, and that NASA did not properly account for the cost savings.

Legal Arguments

SpaceX's protest challenged NASA's evaluation under its Launch Services Program. The company suggested that NASA placed too much weight on ULA's record or unique capabilities and not enough on price. ULA and NASA, meanwhile, emphasized the mission's "extremely narrow launch window" in October 2021 and the need for absolute schedule certainty. ULA's Atlas V had a long track record of reliability and on-time performance, which NASA saw as critical to avoid missing Lucy's one-time planetary alignment. Any launch delay could have pushed the mission to the next window years later, potentially adding mission costs that might outweigh SpaceX's cheaper launch bid.

Outcome

Before GAO could rule, SpaceX withdrew its protest after about two months. By April 2019, SpaceX had dropped the challenge, likely recognizing NASA's justification regarding schedule risk (or for other strategic reasons). The GAO case was dismissed, and NASA's award to ULA stood. Lucy successfully launched on a ULA Atlas V in October 2021 as planned. The protest's withdrawal meant that there was no formal GAO decision on the merits, but effectively, NASA prevailed, and no contract rebid occurred.

Canceled Sole-Source Contract— Kistler Aerospace (2004)

Parties and Context

In 2004, NASA made an attempt to sole-source a contract for commercial launch services to a start-up called Kistler Aerospace. The deal, worth $277 million, was intended to help demonstrate a private rocket for ISS resupply. Kistler, however, was a financially troubled company (it had filed for bankruptcy in 2003) and was staffed by several former NASA officials. NASA's unusual move to award a noncompetitive contract to Kistler raised concerns among other aerospace companies and watchdog groups.

Nature of the Dispute

Competing companies that were excluded from this opportunity, as well as organizations like Citizens Against Government Waste, protested that NASA was trying to "pull a fast one" by bypassing open competition. They pointed out that other firms were interested in the project and that NASA had rejected them in favor of Kistler without a full competition. Given Kistler's shaky financial status and failure to deliver a working vehicle despite years of effort, critics argued that the sole-source award looked like a questionable favor to a company of ex-NASA employees.

Legal Arguments and Outcome

Protests were filed with the GAO in early 2004,[23] challenging NASA's justification for the noncompetitive award. In response to the scrutiny, NASA yanked the sole-source notice on June 23, 2004, before it could turn into a protracted legal battle. Essentially, NASA canceled the planned Kistler contract and proceeded to seek competitive proposals. (This incident foreshadowed NASA's later COTS program—NASA opened a competition and eventually funded SpaceX and Kistler's successor, RpK 2006, although Kistler ultimately failed to meet milestones and was replaced by Orbital.) The quick cancelation in 2004 meant that no court case ensued, but it stands as a notable procurement dispute where GAO pressure forced NASA to backtrack.

These few examples demonstrate a perhaps unintended consequence of private competition for government missions; a near universal response of litigation to an unfavorable proposal evaluation, with accompanying stop-work orders and increased mission schedule risk.

Spacehab Versus NASA—Columbia Disaster Claim (2003–2007)

Parties and Context

Spacehab, Inc. was a NASA contractor that provided a pressurized research module carried aboard the Space Shuttle Columbia on mission STS-107. When Columbia tragically broke apart on reentry in February 2003, Spacehab's module was destroyed along with the shuttle and crew. In 2004, Spacehab filed a formal claim and then a lawsuit against NASA seeking $87.7 million in damages for the loss of its Research Double Module. The claim was based on the contract terms and indemnification provisions for payload loss.[24]

Nature of the Dispute

Spacehab argued that under its contract or under the law, NASA was liable for the value of the module that was lost in the performance of the mission. Initially, Spacehab pursued the matter as a contract claim (through the Armed Services Board of Contract Appeals [ASBCA]) and also filed a lawsuit under the Federal Tort Claims Act for negligence, seeking recovery of roughly $79.7 million (the insured value not covered by NASA's initial payout). Essentially, Spacehab sought to be made whole for the hardware loss, beyond what insurance and NASA's limited reimbursement covered.

Legal Proceedings

NASA acknowledged some liability but calculated a much lower amount. In October 2004, NASA paid Spacehab $8.2 million (including interest) as the extent of its obligation for the lost module. Unsatisfied, Spacehab pressed on: it appealed the contracting officer's decision to the ASBCA and simultaneously filed a separate tort claim for additional damages. The legal debate likely centered on contract clauses about risk assumed by the contractor versus NASA, and whether NASA had been negligent in the events leading to the Columbia accident.

Outcome

After several years, Spacehab decided to withdraw its litigation against NASA. In February 2007, Spacehab moved to dismiss all claims with prejudice, effectively dropping the case. NASA did not pay more than the $8.2 million it had already provided. Spacehab stated that maintaining a good relationship with its largest customer (NASA) and focusing on new business outweighed the uncertain benefits of continuing the legal fight. In the end, Spacehab absorbed the rest of the financial loss. This case highlights a contract performance dispute in which a contractor sought compensation for mission-related losses and ultimately settled for a fraction of the claim, rather than prolonging a battle with NASA.

Contract Protests

The government is required by law (again, as of this writing, the ongoing enforcement of federal law is a bit uncertain) to objectively evaluate proposals by comparing the offered work to the requirements and selection criteria provided. When a bidder feels that this has not happened (or has a bottomless war chest), they are usually entitled to file a protest. Here are a few examples.

High-Profile NASA Contract
Award Protests (2005–2025)

Over the past two decades, several major NASA contract awards have been challenged through formal bid protests. Prominent aerospace companies such as SpaceX, Blue Origin, Boeing, Lockheed Martin, and Northrop Grumman have been involved in disputes over big-ticket NASA programs. These protests are typically filed with the GAO as a first step, and in some cases, escalated to the U.S. Court of Federal Claims. In the following, we outline some of the most high-profile NASA contract award protests of the last 20 years, including the contracts in question, the companies involved, the basis of each protest, and how each was ultimately resolved.

GOES-R Weather Satellite Contract (2008–2009)

Contract in Dispute

In late 2008, NASA (in cooperation with NOAA) awarded Lockheed Martin a $1.1 billion contract to build the next-generation GOES-R series of geostationary weather satellites. Boeing was the losing bidder on this high-profile satellite procurement. Believing its proposal had been superior under NASA's evaluation criteria, Boeing filed a bid protest with the GAO on December 15, 2008.[25]

Basis of Protest

Boeing's protest contended that NASA's source selection was flawed and did not follow the stated evaluation criteria. Boeing argued that it had offered a "superior proposal" yet lost, suggesting that NASA had "inexplicably" altered the evaluation process in a way that unfairly favored Lockheed Martin. In May 2009, during the protest, Boeing publicly accused NASA of making unexplained changes in how proposals were assessed after initial evaluations were complete. The implication was that NASA may have adjusted its scoring or requirements in Lockheed's favor or undervalued Boeing's strengths. Boeing sought a reevaluation or reversal of the award, maintaining that if the criteria were properly applied, its offering should have won.

Outcome

The GOES-R protest concluded without a GAO ruling on the merits, because NASA undertook a voluntary corrective action—essentially a reevaluation of the proposals—and ultimately upheld its original decision to award the contract to Lockheed Martin. Following this reaffirmation by NASA, Boeing withdrew its GAO protest in July 2009. In a statement, Boeing said it decided to withdraw after *"gaining additional insight into the reevaluation process," and while Boeing continues to believe its proposal was strong, it accepted NASA's decision. No contract modifications were announced as a result of the protest; Lockheed Martin retained the GOES-R contract award, and work resumed (in GAO's records, the protest was dismissed due to the withdrawal). This case underscored that even if a company perceives an evaluative disparity, a protest may be dropped if the agency reexamines the decision and stands firm—in this instance, no legal body overturned NASA's award, and Lockheed proceeded to build the GOES-R satellites.

Why It Matters: Where Spending Authority Comes From

All of NASA's power to spend money ultimately traces back to congressional authorization; whether the NASA Authorization Act of 1957 or later actions. We are learning in Summer 2025 that authority is subject to Executive Branch priorities even lacking a formal federal budget, as NASA is moving to implement the President's budget request before it is official. Savvy organizations will "read the tea leaves" to prepare to ride the waves or weather the storms of such variations in federal power distribution.

Story Time 2: 100-Year Starship, Getting Drunk With Levar Burton

> My first opportunity to create my own project came in a very unusual form. DARPA, the Defense Advanced Research Projects Agency, had created a project called the 100-Year Starship. This was in 2011 and the goal was to explore what it would take to design a starship capable

(Continued)

(*Continued*)

of human transportation to another star within 100 years. I had no idea how bizarre and unusual this was when I saw it, but I jumped on it right away. It turned into a fascinating exercise that was ultimately unsuccessful, although I came in second out of about 30 proposals. It gave me the opportunity to learn an enormous amount about how NASA works, how the federal government works and studying other organizations with a very, very long time horizon, such as the Catholic Church and National Geographic, both of which have multiple decade-long missions and projects. I also got to attend several fascinating conferences, where I saw both incredibly revolutionary work and incredibly sophisticated scams and fabrications. I also got to drink with actor Levar Burton at a bar in Texas talking about Star Trek, which is a career highlight.

CHAPTER 3

How It Is

NASA's current activities should be divided into two main sections: human exploration and robotic exploration.

Human Exploration

Technical Architecture and Components

At the heart of the Artemis program is the Space Launch System (SLS), which is described as the most powerful rocket in the world. Standing 322 feet tall (98 meters), this massive launch vehicle consists of a core stage, upper stage, and twin five-segment solid rocket boosters capable of delivering unprecedented payloads beyond Earth orbit. The SLS represents decades of rocket engineering knowledge combined into a single launch system specifically designed to enable deep space exploration.

The Orion spacecraft serves as the crew vehicle for Artemis missions, designed to carry up to four astronauts to lunar orbit and back. Larger than the Apollo command modules, Orion incorporates modern life support systems, radiation protection, and navigation technology to safely transport astronauts on their multiweek journeys. The spacecraft's heat shield must withstand temperatures approaching 5,000 degrees Fahrenheit during Earth reentry, making it a critical safety component for crew survival.

For sustained lunar operations, NASA has incorporated the Gateway into its architecture—a small space station orbiting the Moon where astronauts will prepare for surface missions. This orbital platform will serve as a staging point for lunar landings, scientific research, and potentially as a waystation for future Mars missions. From Gateway, crews will utilize a specialized human landing system to travel to and from the lunar surface, allowing for multiple surface expeditions without requiring a complete Earth return between missions. As of June 2025, it is unclear whether the Gateway station will remain in the final Artemis architecture.

The propulsion systems powering these vehicles have required extensive development and testing. In April 2024, NASA achieved a significant milestone with the completion of a critical certification test series for the RS-25 engines that will power future Artemis missions. These engines, produced by Aerojet Rocketdyne (an L3Harris Technologies company), underwent full-duration hot fire testing at NASA's Stennis Space Center in Mississippi, validating their readiness for upcoming flights beginning with Artemis.

The Artemis Mission Roadmap

NASA established a three-phase approach for the initial Artemis missions, creating a progressive sequence of increasingly complex operations to ensure safety and mission success. This methodical strategy mirrors the approach used during the Apollo program, where capabilities were demonstrated incrementally before attempting a lunar landing.

The first phase, Artemis I, was designed as an uncrewed test flight to validate the performance of both the SLS rocket and the Orion spacecraft in the deep space environment. This critical mission would demonstrate the vehicle's ability to reach lunar orbit, perform maneuvers around the Moon, and safely return to Earth with a precise splashdown. The mission would also deploy several small scientific satellites (cubesats) to perform supplementary experiments and technology demonstrations.

Following the successful completion of Artemis I, the Artemis II mission would carry the first four Artemis astronauts on a crewed lunar flyby. This mission would take humans farther from Earth than ever before, testing all of Orion's life support and crew systems during an approximately 10-day journey. While not including a lunar landing component, Artemis II represents a crucial step in validating human-rated systems before attempting a surface mission.

The culmination of this initial sequence, Artemis III, will return humans to the lunar surface for the first time since Apollo 17 departed in December 1972. This historic mission will land the first woman and the next man on the Moon's south pole region, an area of significant scientific interest due to the potential presence of water ice and other resources. The mission architecture involves multiple components working in concert, including the SLS, Orion, Gateway (potentially), and the human landing system.

Artemis I: The Successful First Step

After years of development and testing, NASA successfully launched Artemis I at 01:47 a.m. EST on November 16, 2022, from Launch Complex 39B at Kennedy Space Center in Florida. This uncrewed mission marked the operational debut of the SLS and demonstrated the integration of its major components. The powerful rocket performed as expected, sending the Orion spacecraft on its trajectory toward the Moon.

During its 25.5-day mission, Orion traveled approximately 1.4 million miles (2.3 million kilometers), circumnavigating the Moon and testing crucial systems in the actual space environment. The spacecraft executed a series of engine burns to adjust its trajectory, demonstrated its communication and navigation capabilities, and collected valuable data on radiation exposure and thermal conditions. This extended journey allowed NASA to evaluate how the vehicle's systems performed during prolonged exposure to deep space.

After completing its lunar operations, Orion began its return journey to Earth, culminating in a critical test of its heat shield during high-speed atmospheric reentry. The mission concluded with a successful splashdown in the Pacific Ocean off the coast of Mexico's Baja Peninsula at 12:40 p.m. EST on December 11, 2022[1]. Recovery teams successfully retrieved the spacecraft, allowing engineers to examine its condition after the demanding journey.

Post mission analysis revealed an unexpected issue that would significantly impact the program's future timeline. Engineers discovered that charred bits of the heat shield had broken off during reentry—a concerning finding for a component critical to crew safety. This anomaly prompted NASA to initiate a thorough investigation, as the heat shield must protect future astronauts from temperatures approaching 5,000 degrees Fahrenheit during their return to Earth. This would turn out to be a major issue that continues to plague the program at the time of this writing, with the most recent decision made to adjust the reentry trajectory to reduce heating on the vehicle. This is a very unusual step and represents the power of these contracts (NASA would rather change the path of the vehicle than fight with contractors over heat shield performance). It is a safety issue and the wrong decision in this author's opinion. See "Mission Out of Control" by Astronaut Charles Camarda for much more.

Challenges and Timeline Adjustments

Like many earlier ambitious space programs, the Artemis program has faced numerous technical challenges that have necessitated timeline adjustments. These changes reflect NASA's commitment to safety over schedule, particularly when human lives will be at stake during crewed missions.

The original timeline for Artemis missions was projected for Artemis II to launch in late 2024, followed by Artemis III in 2025. However, various technical issues and development challenges prompted NASA to revise this schedule. In January 2024, NASA announced the first major delay, pushing Artemis II to September 2025, citing the need for additional preparation time.

On December 5, 2024, NASA Administrator Bill Nelson announced a more substantial revision to the program timeline during a press conference addressing the heat shield investigation and other technical concerns.[26] This announcement further delayed Artemis II until no earlier than April 2026, with Artemis III correspondingly pushed to mid-2027. These adjustments resulted primarily from the discovery of heat shield issues during the Artemis I mission, with NASA requiring additional time to ensure that the Orion capsule could safely return crews from lunar distances.

Despite these delays, then-Administrator Nelson expressed confidence that the revised timeline would still enable American astronauts to reach the lunar surface before China's stated goal of landing its own astronauts on the Moon by 2030. This acknowledgment of international competition echoes the space race dynamics of the Apollo era, though with a more collaborative international framework through initiatives like the Artemis Accords. As 2025 passes along with major Chinese achievements[27] and continued uncertainty from NASA, this outcome looks less and less likely.

The Artemis Accords: An International Framework

Recognizing that sustainable space exploration requires international cooperation, NASA, in coordination with the U.S. Department of State, established the Artemis Accords in 2020 with seven other initial signatory nations. These accords provide a common set of principles to enhance the governance of civil exploration and use of outer space, creating a framework for peaceful collaboration beyond Earth.[28]

The Artemis Accords reinforce signatories' commitment to existing space treaties, including the Outer Space Treaty, the Registration Convention, and the Rescue and Return Agreement, while also establishing new norms for responsible behavior in space exploration. This approach acknowledges the evolved nature of space activities since those foundational treaties were established in the 1960s and 1970s.

Core principles of the Artemis Accords include commitments to peaceful purposes, transparency, interoperability of systems, emergency assistance to astronauts in distress, and proper registration of space objects. These foundational elements create a cooperative framework that respects both existing international law and the practical realities of modern space operations.

The Accords also address newer concerns such as the preservation of historically significant sites and artifacts in space, the utilization of space resources, the deconfliction of activities through "safety zones," and the mitigation of orbital debris. These provisions demonstrate forethought regarding potential conflicts or environmental concerns as lunar activities increase in the coming decades.

A particularly innovative concept within the Accords is the establishment of temporary "safety zones" around operational sites, with signatories committing to coordination to avoid harmful interference while respecting the principles of free access under the Outer Space Treaty. This approach attempts to balance operational safety with the legal principle that no nation may claim sovereignty over celestial bodies, creating a practical framework for multiple entities operating in close proximity on the lunar surface.

Future Prospects and Significance

Despite the technical challenges and schedule adjustments, the Artemis program represents humanity's most comprehensive attempt to establish a sustainable presence beyond Earth orbit. The program's ambitious scope extends far beyond the initial landing missions, with plans for regular sorties to different lunar regions and eventually the establishment of a permanent outpost.

The technological developments stemming from Artemis have applications beyond lunar exploration. NASA explicitly frames the Moon as a proving ground for technologies and operational concepts that will eventually enable human exploration of Mars. Systems such as long-duration life support, radiation protection, and resource utilization developed for lunar applications will directly transfer to future Mars mission architectures, making Artemis an essential stepping stone in humanity's expansion into the solar system.

Scientific discoveries from Artemis missions promise to revolutionize our understanding of lunar formation, evolution, and resource potential. The focus on the lunar south pole region, with its permanently shadowed craters potentially containing water ice, could provide insights into both practical resource utilization and fundamental questions about the Moon's history. These scientific returns justify the significant investment in the program, independent of its human exploration achievements.

Perhaps most significantly, Artemis initially represented a more inclusive vision of space exploration than its predecessors. By explicitly committing to land the first woman and person of color on the lunar surface, NASA acknowledged that humanity's greatest exploratory achievements should reflect humanity's diversity. This inclusive approach extends to international participation through the Artemis Accords, creating a framework where multiple nations can contribute to and benefit from lunar exploration. Whether this overcommitment to diversity survives the new NASA administrator's review (as of this writing, there is still no new administrator) remains to be seen.

The NASA Artemis program stands as a testament to humanity's enduring desire to explore beyond our home planet while incorporating lessons learned from previous space endeavors. From its establishment during the Trump administration to its current progress under subsequent leadership, Artemis has maintained its core vision of returning humans to the lunar surface while expanding its scope to include sustainable presence and preparation for Mars.

The successful completion of Artemis I in December 2022 marked a crucial milestone, demonstrating the capabilities of the SLS and Orion spacecraft while revealing areas requiring additional refinement before carrying human crews. The resulting timeline adjustments, while disappointing to space enthusiasts eager to see humans return to the Moon, reflect NASA's appropriate prioritization of safety over schedule, particularly regarding the critical heat shield components necessary for crew survival.

As NASA works toward the April 2026 launch of Artemis II and the mid-2027 landing of Artemis III, the program continues to develop the technologies, international partnerships, and operational experience necessary for sustained lunar exploration. With the framework established by the Artemis Accords, this new era of lunar exploration promises to be more collaborative and inclusive than previous space endeavors, potentially creating a model for how humanity might cooperatively expand into the solar system in the coming decades.

All of the above represents the official story about the Artemis program, full of flowery, ambitious language steeped in traditional American values. Much of that is true, but it should also be noted that enormous amounts of money are at stake.

NASA's Artemis Program: A Comprehensive Analysis of Major Contracts

The Artemis program represents one of NASA's most ambitious endeavors since the Apollo missions, aiming to return humans to the lunar surface and establish a sustainable presence on the Moon. To achieve these lofty goals, NASA relies on an extensive network of contractors developing everything from launch vehicles to lunar rovers. This program has created a significant economic ecosystem, with NASA having obligated approximately $40 billion to 860 contractors from fiscal years 2012 to 2022. As of March 2025, the contracting landscape continues to evolve as NASA prepares for upcoming Artemis missions. This report examines the major contracts underpinning the Artemis program, detailing their values, purposes, and the companies responsible for delivering these critical components of America's return to the Moon.

Prime Contractor Infrastructure

The backbone of the Artemis program consists of 17 major prime contractors holding 23 separate contracts with a combined value exceeding $63 billion as of April 2023.[29] These contracts cover the development and production of the program's essential systems: the Orion spacecraft, SLS, exploration ground systems, and lunar landing vehicles. The contract structure reflects NASA's approach to managing complex development projects, with a mix of cost-reimbursement and fixed-price contracts depending on the maturity of the technology and associated risks.

Orion Spacecraft Contracts

The Orion spacecraft serves as the crew vehicle for Artemis missions, designed to carry astronauts to lunar orbit and safely return them to Earth. Two major contracts with Lockheed Martin form the foundation of Orion development and production:

Lockheed Martin received a cost-reimbursement contract valued at $15 billion (over many years)[30] for Orion development, making it one of the largest single contracts in the Artemis program. This contract covers the design, testing, and initial production of the spacecraft. The development contract is complemented by the Orion Production and Operations Contract, also awarded to Lockheed Martin, with a value of $4.9 billion.[31] This second cost-reimbursement contract focuses on serial production of Orion capsules for multiple Artemis missions, ensuring a sustainable pipeline of crew vehicles as the program progresses.

The cost-reimbursement structure of both Orion contracts reflects the technical complexity and developmental nature of human-rated spacecraft. Under this arrangement, NASA bears most of the financial risk but maintains significant control over design decisions and manufacturing processes to ensure that astronaut safety remains paramount.

Space Launch System Contracts

The SLS, NASA's super-heavy lift rocket designed to propel Orion beyond Earth orbit, relies on multiple contractors developing different components of the launch vehicle. Boeing serves as the primary contractor for the

SLS core stages and Exploration Upper Stage under a cost-reimbursement contract valued at $9.7 billion.[32] This contract covers the design, development, and production of the massive core stage that houses the rocket's main propellant tanks and engines.

Boeing holds an additional fixed-price contract worth $1 billion for the Interim Cryogenic Propulsion Stage 5, which serves as the upper stage for initial SLS missions before the more powerful Exploration Upper Stage becomes available. The difference in contract types—cost-reimbursement for the core stage versus fixed-price for the upper stage—likely reflects the varying degrees of technical risk and development complexity associated with each component.

Propulsion systems for the SLS rely heavily on Aerojet Rocketdyne, which holds two significant contracts. The first, valued at $580.9 million, covers the adaptation of existing RS-25 engines (originally used on the Space Shuttle) for SLS requirements. The second, worth $3.6 billion,[33] funds the restart of RS-25 engine production, as the initial supply of repurposed Space Shuttle engines will be depleted after the first four Artemis missions.

Northrop Grumman contributes to SLS through a $4.4 billion cost-reimbursement contract for the development and production of the rocket's five-segment solid rocket boosters. These boosters, evolved from Space Shuttle technology, provide the majority of thrust during the initial launch phase. Teledyne Brown Engineering rounds out the SLS contractor team with a $350 million cost-reimbursement contract for the Launch Vehicle Stage Adapter, which connects the core stage to the upper stage.

A notable addition to the SLS contractor team is Dynetics, which is developing the Universal Stage Adapter. This component will be used on later SLS configurations (if the program survives) to connect the larger Exploration Upper Stage to the Orion spacecraft and provide space for secondary payloads. The value of this contract is not public information as of the time of this writing.

Recent Contract Awards

Beyond the established prime contracts for Orion and SLS, NASA continues to expand the Artemis contractor base as the program evolves toward sustained lunar operations. In early 2025, NASA awarded contracts to nine companies under the Next Space Technologies for Exploration Partnerships (NextSTEP) Appendix R contracts, with a combined value of $24 million. These contracts focus on developing capabilities to address challenges specific to the lunar environment, aligning with NASA's broader Moon to Mars Architecture.

According to Nujoud Merancy, deputy associate administrator in NASA's Strategy and Architecture Office, "These contract awards are the catalyst for developing critical capabilities for the Artemis missions and the everyday needs of astronauts for long-term exploration on the lunar surface."

In April 2024, NASA took a significant step toward establishing mobility systems on the lunar surface by awarding contracts to three companies for Lunar Terrain Vehicle (LTV) development. Intuitive Machines of Houston, Lunar Outpost of Golden, Colorado, and Venturi Astrolab of Hawthorne, California, received "feasibility" contracts to spend 12 months perfecting their rover designs before NASA conducts a formal competition to select a single contractor for full development, worth a billion dollars. The milestone-based Lunar Terrain Vehicle Services contract has a maximum potential value of $4.6 billion, reflecting the long-term nature of lunar surface operations and the importance of mobility systems for exploring the challenging lunar terrain.

These recent contract awards demonstrate NASA's evolving approach to Artemis procurement, with an increasing focus on services-based and milestone-based contracts rather than traditional hardware development agreements. This shift aligns with NASA's stated goal of establishing a sustainable lunar presence where commercial partners play increasingly significant roles.

Contract Management Approach

NASA's contracting strategy for Artemis reflects a balance between different procurement approaches based on technological maturity and risk profiles. Of the 23 major contracts identified in the NASA Office of Inspector General report, 11 use cost-reimbursement structures while 12 employ fixed-price arrangements. This distribution indicates NASA's tailored approach to managing different aspects of the program.

Under cost-reimbursement contracts, which cover most of the core Artemis vehicle development, NASA "approves all designs, manages all development and schedules, and owns the vehicle after delivery by the contractor." While this approach gives NASA maximum control over design decisions and final products, it also means that "the majority of the cost, schedule, and outcome risks are borne by the federal government."

In contrast, fixed-price contracts "provide a set price that does not change if the contractor's costs increase during the period of performance due to inflation or supply chain issues, resulting in lower risk to the government from subcontractors and suppliers." NASA's increasing use of fixed-price arrangements for more mature technologies or service-based elements of the Artemis program suggests an evolution in procurement strategy as the program matures.

The distribution of contract types also reflects NASA's recognition of the complex supply chain supporting Artemis. While the agency has direct contracts with 860 contractors, the vast majority of Artemis work occurs through subcontracts managed by the major prime contractors. This multilayered supply chain creates both opportunities and challenges for NASA's contract management approach.

The Artemis Accords Framework

While not contracts in the traditional sense, the Artemis Accords represent an important framework for international cooperation that complements NASA's commercial contracting strategy. As of January 21, 2025, 53 countries have signed these accords, including 27 in Europe, 9 in Asia, 7 in South America, 5 in North America, 3 in Africa, and 2 in Oceania. Finland became the most recent signatory on January 21, 2025.

The Accords, drafted by NASA and the U.S. Department of State, establish principles for civil exploration and peaceful use of the Moon, Mars, and other astronomical objects. They are explicitly grounded in the United Nations Outer Space Treaty of 1967 and other major space law conventions, providing a framework for international participation in lunar exploration activities.

While the Accords themselves don't directly involve financial contracts, they create the diplomatic foundation for potential international contributions to Artemis missions. Countries that sign the Accords may choose to directly participate in Artemis program activities or simply commit to the principles for responsible lunar exploration outlined in the agreement. This framework potentially expands the pool of resources available for Artemis beyond NASA's direct contracts with U.S. companies.

Economic Significance and Future Outlook

The scale of Artemis contracts—exceeding $63 billion for major prime contractors alone—highlights the program's significant economic impact. These contracts support jobs across the aerospace industry and its supply chain, with benefits extending well beyond the prime contractors to hundreds of subcontractors and suppliers.

Recent contract awards for lunar rovers and other capabilities suggest that NASA continues to expand the Artemis contractor base as the program advances toward sustained lunar operations. The maximum potential value of $4.6 billion for the Lunar Terrain Vehicle Services contract[34] indicates NASA's commitment to long-term lunar exploration and the development of infrastructure to support an extended human presence on the Moon.

As Nujoud Merancy noted regarding the recent NextSTEP contracts, "The strong response to our request for proposals is a testament to the interest in human exploration and the growing deep-space economy." This growing commercial interest in lunar activities suggests that Artemis contracts may increasingly serve as catalysts for broader commercial space activities beyond NASA's specific mission requirements.

The Artemis program represents a massive undertaking supported by an extensive network of contracts with aerospace companies across the United States. These contracts, valued at tens of billions of dollars, fund the development of spacecraft, launch vehicles, and surface systems necessary for returning humans to the Moon and establishing a sustainable lunar presence.

NASA's contracting approach balances traditional cost-reimbursement contracts for complex development work with newer fixed-price and services-based models for more mature capabilities. This hybrid procurement strategy reflects both the technical challenges of lunar exploration and NASA's desire to foster commercial capabilities that can support long-term space exploration goals.

As the Artemis program progresses toward the first crewed lunar landing since Apollo, the contracting landscape will likely continue to evolve, with increasing emphasis on sustainable operations and commercial partnerships. The economic ecosystem created by these contracts extends far beyond the major prime contractors, supporting a complex supply chain of aerospace companies and creating a foundation for potential commercial lunar activities in the coming decades.

Speculation: How the Second Trump Administration Might Change the Game

The future of NASA's Artemis program stands at a critical crossroads following the inauguration of President Trump for his second term. While Trump's first administration established Artemis in 2017 with the goal of returning humans to the lunar surface, recent signals suggest potentially dramatic shifts in America's space exploration priorities. This section examines the current speculation surrounding NASA's flagship human spaceflight program and analyzes the various indicators pointing to possible changes under the second Trump administration. Echoing the dual purposes of Artemis as an extension of American leadership and an enormous financial impact on contractors, their employees, and their local communities, the current dynamics indicate major imminent changes.

Leadership Changes and Early Signals

The transition period has already produced notable shifts in NASA's leadership structure that may foreshadow changes to the Artemis program. On January 20, 2025, President Trump's first day back in office, he made the unusual decision to designate Janet Petro, Kennedy Space Center director, as Acting NASA Administrator rather than following the established order of succession that would have placed Associate Administrator Jim Free in the role.

This departure from standard protocol took many observers by surprise and potentially signals a desire to install leadership more aligned with the new administration's vision. The move circumvented an executive order dating back to January 2009 that codified the succession process, suggesting an intentional break from established practice.

Further reinforcing speculation about leadership changes, NASA abruptly announced the retirement of longtime associate administrator Jim Free, effective February 22, 2025. No official reason was provided for Free's departure after his 30-year rise to NASA's top civil service position. Significantly, Free was a strong advocate for the Artemis program and its incremental approach of returning to the Moon before attempting Mars missions.

In another signal of potential directional change, President Trump has tapped private astronaut and e-payments billionaire Jared Isaacman as his nominee for NASA Administrator. Isaacman, who has flown to space twice with SpaceX, is considered a close ally of Elon Musk, suggesting further alignment between NASA and SpaceX's priorities. During the writing of this book, Isaacman was removed from consideration, and as of late June 2025, no alternative or replacement has been identified.

The Musk Factor: Increasing Influence on Space Policy

Perhaps the most significant indicator of potential changes to Artemis comes from the growing influence of Elon Musk in the new administration. Musk played an active role in Trump's election campaign and has been appointed coleader of the newly established "Department of Government Efficiency" (DOGE), giving him substantial influence over federal spending priorities. That Musk seems to have withdrawn from active involvement with DOGE (having prioritized the decimation of the agencies investigating his companies) does not necessarily mean he has lost interest in space exploration.

Musk has been explicit about his preference for Mars exploration over lunar missions. On January 3, 2025, he stated on his social media platform X: "We're going straight to Mars. The moon is a distraction." This direct statement from a key presidential adviser has fueled speculation about a potential redirection of NASA's human spaceflight program away from the Moon-first approach.

Musk has also publicly criticized the current Artemis architecture as "extremely inefficient," suggesting that he may advocate for significant restructuring of the program if not an outright change in destination.

His company, SpaceX, holds major contracts within the Artemis program, including a $2.9 billion award for the Artemis III human landing system and an additional $1.15 billion for Artemis IV. Despite these existing investments in lunar missions, Musk's stated preference for Mars suggests possible tension between his commercial interests and personal vision.

In mid-June 2025, Musk and President Trump seemed to experience a major disagreement, with Musk leaving his government position. It remains to be seen what will emerge from the chaos.

Signs of Potential Program Restructuring

Concrete evidence of potential changes to Artemis emerged in February 2025 when Boeing announced plans to lay off approximately 400 employees working on the SLS rocket program.[35] Boeing explicitly stated that this decision was made to "align with revisions to the Artemis program and cost expectation," indicating that the company anticipates significant changes to NASA's lunar exploration plans.

Keith Cowing, a former NASA scientist and founder of NASA Watch, interpreted Boeing's decision as the company "seeing the writing on the wall" regarding SLS's future. He suggested that the massive rocket is "likely to fly only one or two missions, or they'll cancel it outright." SLS has long faced criticism for its extreme costs and development delays, making it a potential target for budget cuts under an administration focused on efficiency.

Beyond SLS, other components of the Artemis architecture may also face scrutiny. The lunar Gateway space station, which would serve as a staging point for surface missions, could be "in the new administration's crosshairs over cost and delays." Any decision to cancel or significantly alter Gateway would have international ramifications, as partners including the European Space Agency, Canadian Space Agency, and Japan Aerospace Exploration Agency are already developing hardware for the project.

Mars Ambitions Versus Lunar Foundations

President Trump's own statements have reinforced speculation about a potential shift from lunar to Martian exploration. In his January 2025 inauguration speech, he "vowed that the U.S. would 'plant the stars and stripes on the planet Mars,'" signaling a commitment to reaching the Red Planet during his term. While this statement doesn't explicitly contradict the Moon-first approach, it emphasizes Mars as the primary goal rather than sustainable lunar exploration.

This potential redirection would echo aspects of President Obama's space policy, which aimed for a Mars orbit mission by the 2030s while deemphasizing lunar landings. That approach faced significant congressional pushback at the time, suggesting that a similar reaction could occur if Trump attempts to bypass the Moon entirely.

Musk's timeline for Mars exploration is notably aggressive, with plans to send five uncrewed Starships to Mars in 2026 and, if successful, crewed missions by 2028. Space policy experts generally consider this schedule highly unrealistic given the technical challenges, radiation exposure risks, and funding requirements, but it aligns with Trump's apparent desire for a Mars achievement during his presidency. These same risk factors would apply regardless of leadership, but some things should not be rushed.

Congressional Constraints and Geopolitical Considerations

Despite the administration's apparent interest in prioritizing Mars, significant obstacles may prevent dramatic changes to the Artemis program. Chief among these is Congress, which controls NASA's funding and has historically supported the Moon-first approach.

Marcia Smith, a veteran space policy expert with 40 years of experience, predicted: "The new Trump Administration might try to skip the moon and go straight to Mars, but I expect they would encounter the same backlash from Congress as Obama did when he proposed that in 2010." She emphasized that "Congress wants a moon-to-Mars program, not one or the other," suggesting that legislators would resist any attempt to abandon lunar objectives entirely.

The House Science, Space, and Technology Committee scheduled a hearing titled "Step by Step: The Artemis Program and NASA's Path to Human Exploration of the Moon, Mars, and Beyond" for February 26, 2025, indicating congressional interest in maintaining the current approach. Notably, this hearing did not include witnesses from the Trump administration, suggesting that it may serve primarily as a platform for reinforcing congressional support for the existing program.

Geopolitical considerations are also a factor in decisions about lunar exploration. China continues developing its own lunar program, the International Lunar Research Station (ILRS), and is seeking international partners. Any U.S. decision to abandon lunar objectives could create opportunities for China to establish leadership in cislunar space, with potential national security implications.

Continued Development Amid Uncertainty

Despite the speculation about program changes, NASA continues to work on Artemis-related projects. On January 23, 2025, the agency announced contracts to nine companies under the Next Space Technologies for Exploration Partnerships (NextSTEP) Appendix R program, with a combined value of $24 million. These contracts focus on developing capabilities for lunar surface logistics, though they may not result in operational hardware for years.

Nujoud Merancy, deputy associate administrator in NASA's Strategy and Architecture Office, characterized these awards as "an important step to a sustainable return to the moon," suggesting at least some parts of the agency continue operating under the assumption that lunar exploration remains the priority. However, the focus on far-future logistics studies rather than near-term mission components could indicate hesitation in committing resources to immediate lunar plans during this period of policy uncertainty.

In April 2024, NASA awarded contracts to three companies (Intuitive Machines, Lunar Outpost, and Venturi Astrolab) for LTV development, with these companies now working on 12-month feasibility studies before a formal competition for full development. This lunar rover program has a maximum potential value of $4.6 billion, representing a significant long-term investment in surface exploration capabilities that could be at risk if priorities shift.

The future direction of NASA's Artemis program remains uncertain as the second Trump administration establishes its space policy priorities. Multiple signals—including leadership changes, Elon Musk's increasing influence, contractor workforce reductions, and presidential rhetoric focusing on Mars—suggest potential shifts away from the current lunar-focused approach. However, congressional support for the Moon-first strategy and international commitments may constrain dramatic policy changes.

The coming months will likely bring greater clarity as the administration formally establishes its space policy through appointments, budget requests, and potential new space policy directives. The existing Artemis program represents billions in contracts and international agreements that cannot be easily unwound, but history has shown that presidential transitions often bring significant changes to NASA's human spaceflight goals.

As this situation continues to evolve, the fundamental tension appears to be between those advocating for the incremental, sustainable approach of establishing lunar infrastructure before attempting Mars and those preferring to bypass the Moon in favor of a more direct path to the Red Planet. This debate will likely shape American space policy throughout the second Trump administration, with significant implications for NASA, its commercial partners, and international space cooperation.

NASA Science Mission Directorate: Current Operational Science Missions and Associated Contracts

The NASA Science Mission Directorate (SMD) oversees an extensive portfolio of scientific missions that explore Earth, the Sun, our solar system, and the universe beyond. These missions not only advance our scientific understanding but also represent significant business opportunities through various contracts and partnerships. This report provides a comprehensive overview of NASA's ongoing science missions with a particular focus on associated contracts that may interest business-minded readers.

At the time of this writing, there is no 2026 Federal Budget, and the White House proposed budget makes extreme cuts that would render the following section inaccurate. However, the budget negotiations are still ongoing in Congress with a deadline in x. Given that, the following sections represent the last known state of various projects and contracts prior to the 2026 budget discussions.

Overview of the Science Mission Directorate

The SMD manages NASA's scientific exploration through five divisions: Astrophysics, Biological and Physical Sciences, Earth Science, Heliophysics, and Planetary Science. While pursuing groundbreaking scientific discoveries, SMD awards and manages numerous contracts with private companies, academic institutions, and international partners to develop, build, operate, and support these missions.

Astrophysics Division Missions and Contracts

The Astrophysics Division sponsors research to explore the universe beyond our solar system, from exoplanets to the cosmic dawn of the universe itself. Several major contracts support these exploration efforts.

Hubble Space Telescope

The Hubble Space Telescope continues to provide unprecedented views of distant celestial objects more than three decades after its launch. To support this long-running mission, NASA has invested in extended operational contracts:

In 2016, NASA awarded a substantial contract extension to the Association of Universities for Research in Astronomy for continued Hubble science operations support at the Space Telescope Science Institute in Baltimore. This extension increased the contract value by approximately $196.3 million for a total contract value of $2.03 billion,[36] covering operations through June 30, 2021. Subsequent extensions have been awarded to maintain this invaluable scientific asset.

Chandra X-ray Observatory

The Chandra X-ray Observatory continues to provide unique X-ray observations of cosmic phenomena. Its operations are supported through dedicated contracts:

NASA extended its contract with the Smithsonian Astrophysical Observatory in Cambridge, Massachusetts, to provide science and operational support for Chandra. A notable extension in 2002 was valued at $50.75 million for a 11-month period, bringing the total contract value to $298.2 million at that time. More recent extensions have continued to fund the operations of this important observatory.

James Webb Space Telescope

The James Webb Space Telescope (JWST) represents one of NASA's most significant investments in space science infrastructure. The complex mission required numerous contracts:

The JWST spacecraft platform was provided under the NASA contract with Lockheed Martin Missiles and Space in Valley Forge, Pennsylvania. The project implementation included contracts for development, implementation, and maintenance of the telescope's systems. The overall mission involved an intricate web of contractors and subcontractors managing various aspects of the telescope's construction, testing, and operations.

Earth Science Division Missions and Contracts

The Earth Science Division utilizes space-based platforms to monitor our changing planet, supporting climate research, weather forecasting, and environmental management. These missions represent significant procurement opportunities.

Terra and Earth Observation Satellites

The Terra spacecraft, a flagship Earth observation mission, was built by Lockheed Martin Missiles and Space under a NASA contract. The five instruments onboard were procured under separate NASA contracts with various U.S. and international corporations. The total cost was approximately $1.3 billion, including spacecraft, U.S. instruments, and launch vehicle (not including ground system costs or international instrument contributions).

Commercial SmallSat Data Acquisition Program

In a significant move toward leveraging commercial capabilities, NASA awarded positions on a potential $476 million multiple-award contract to eight companies in 2024 to acquire Earth observation data derived from commercially operated small satellites.[37] This indefinite-delivery/indefinite-quantity contract runs through November 15, 2028, and represents a substantial opportunity for providers of Earth observation data.

The awardees include BlackSky Geospatial Solutions, ICEYE US, MDA Geospatial Service, Pixxel Space Technologies, Planet Labs Federal, Satellogic Federal, Teledyne Brown Engineering, and The Tomorrow Companies. This program complements observation data from NASA, other U.S. government agencies, and international partners to support Earth science research and applications.

Heliophysics Division Missions and Contracts

The Heliophysics Division studies the Sun and its influence on the Earth and the solar system. Several contracts support these solar observations and space weather monitoring efforts.

Solar Dynamics Observatory

The Solar Dynamics Observatory (SDO) continues to monitor solar activity and its effects on Earth. In September 2024, NASA awarded a contract extension to Stanford University to continue the mission and services for the Helioseismic and Magnetic Imager (HMI) instrument on SDO. This cost-reimbursement, no-fee contract extension provides for support, operation, and calibration of the HMI instrument, as well as operating and maintaining the Joint Science Operations Center—Science Data Processing facility at Stanford. The extension, running from October 1, 2024, through September 30, 2027, increased the total contract value by about $12.5 million—from $173.84 to $186.34 million.

Planetary Science Division Missions and Contracts

The Planetary Science Division sponsors research to explore our solar system, from nearby Mars to the outer planets and their moons. These ambitious missions require specialized technologies and services.

Mars Sample Return and Dragonfly Missions

NASA has selected Fiber Materials Inc. of Biddeford, Maine, for a contract providing thermal protection systems for three SMD missions: Mars Sample Return (MSR)/Earth Entry Vehicle, MSR Sample Return Lander, and Dragonfly. The contract, which began in January 20, 2022, and runs through January 19, 2026, has a maximum value of $24 million and a minimum order value satisfied with the first order of $635,748.29.

The requirement involves developing specifications for thermal protection system materials and producing the hardware according to NASA's schedule. Fiber Materials will deliver these materials to each project for integration onto the respective spacecraft.

Starlab and Commercial Space Station Development

While not directly under the Planetary Science Division, NASA's broader science mission is supported by initiatives like Starlab. Voyager Space and Northrop Grumman announced a teaming agreement in 2023 to develop fully autonomous rendezvous and docking technology for Northrop Grumman's Cygnus spacecraft and provide cargo resupply services for the Starlab commercial space station. Under this agreement, Northrop Grumman will upgrade its Cygnus cargo vehicle with a fully autonomous docking system to support Starlab missions. The Cygnus spacecraft will deliver pressurized cargo to Starlab over an initial five-year period to support future human spaceflight missions.

NASA's SMD continues to offer substantial business opportunities across its diverse portfolio of science missions. From spacecraft development to instrument construction, mission operations, and data services, companies with relevant capabilities have numerous entry points to participate in these groundbreaking scientific endeavors.

For businesses interested in NASA contracts, monitoring upcoming mission plans, renewal cycles for existing mission operations, and new initiatives like the Commercial SmallSat Data Acquisition Program can reveal valuable opportunities. The trend toward greater commercialization and public–private partnerships, particularly evident in Earth observation and future space station development, suggests expanding prospects for private sector involvement in NASA's science mission activities.

As NASA continues to pursue ambitious goals in space science and exploration, businesses with technological capabilities in areas such as thermal protection systems, autonomous spacecraft operations, sensor development, data processing, and mission operations support will find a robust marketplace for their products and services within the SMD's programs.

Public/Private Exploration

NASA's Robotic Missions in 2025: Commercial Contracts Driving Lunar Exploration

NASA has significantly ramped up its robotic lunar exploration program for 2025, primarily through the Commercial Lunar Payload Services (CLPS) initiative. This ambitious program is sending multiple robotic missions to various regions of the Moon to conduct scientific experiments, test new technologies, and prepare for future human missions under the Artemis program. The CLPS initiative represents a new, supplementary approach to space exploration where NASA contracts private companies to deliver payloads to the lunar surface, creating a sustainable commercial lunar economy while advancing scientific knowledge. In theory, this approach will also lower costs for human exploration efforts by enabling industry at future human destinations.

The Commercial Lunar Payload Services Initiative

The CLPS program was established by NASA to hire private companies to send small robotic landers and rovers to the Moon. The program operates under NASA's SMD in collaboration with the Human Exploration and Operations and Space Technology Mission directorates. CLPS is designed to support the Artemis lunar program by scouting lunar resources, testing in situ resource utilization concepts, and performing lunar science.

The financial structure of the CLPS program is based on indefinite-delivery/indefinite-quantity (IDIQ) contracts with a cumulative maximum value of $2.6 billion through 2028. These contracts cover end-to-end commercial payload delivery services, including payload integration, launch from Earth, landing on the lunar surface, and mission operations. This approach allows NASA to buy fixed-price services between Earth and the lunar surface, leveraging commercial capabilities while focusing on scientific objectives.

The CLPS initiative has already made history with the first landing on the Moon by a commercial company in 2024 through the IM-1 mission. For 2025, NASA has planned multiple CLPS missions at a cadence of approximately two per year. The program currently maintains 11 active contracts with 13 American companies, encompassing a portfolio of 11 lunar deliveries by 5 vendors that will transport more than 50 individual science and technology instruments to lunar orbit and the surface.

Firefly Aerospace's Blue Ghost Mission

One of the most imminent CLPS missions is Firefly Aerospace's Blue Ghost Mission 1, nicknamed "Ghost Riders in the Sky." This mission launched on January 15, 2025, at 1:11 a.m. EST aboard a SpaceX Falcon 9 rocket from Launch Complex 39A at NASA's Kennedy Space Center in Florida. The lander arrived on the Moon on March 2, 2025.

Blue Ghost is carrying 10 NASA science and technology payloads designed to conduct a variety of scientific investigations. The landing target is Mare Crisium, a 300-mile-wide basin located on the Moon's near side that formed from an ancient asteroid impact. This large, dark, basaltic plain will be the site of first-of-their-kind experiments that will deploy after landing to gather crucial data on geophysical characteristics, global navigation, radiation-tolerant computing, and the behavior of lunar regolith.

Among the payloads are technologies specifically designed to study lunar regolith (Moon dust) and understand its interactions with spacecraft and surface equipment. This research is particularly important as the dusty environment was one of the greatest challenges faced by Apollo astronauts and remains a significant concern for future lunar missions.

NASA awarded Firefly Aerospace this delivery contract in February 2021, initially valued at approximately $93.3 million but later modified to $101.5 million.[38] The lander is expected to operate during the daylight hours of one lunar day (approximately 14 Earth days), during which it will collect data about the Moon's surface and how it interacts with the solar wind and Earth's magnetic field. Toward the end of its mission, Blue Ghost 1 will capture images of the lunar sunset and collect data about surface changes that occur at dusk.

Intuitive Machines' IM-2 Mission

Following their successful IM-1 mission, which landed on the Moon in 2024 (though it tipped over after landing), Intuitive Machines is preparing their IM-2 mission as NASA's fourth CLPS flight. This mission is scheduled to launch in February 2025 and aims to land at the Moon's south pole.

The IM-2 spacecraft will target Mons Mouton, a lunar plateau just outside of 5 degrees of the South Pole, making it closer to the pole than any preceding lunar mission. This location is strategically important as the south pole region is believed to contain water ice and other resources that could support future human missions.

The scientific objectives of the IM-2 mission include measuring the regolith's volatiles (delicate chemical compounds) using a drill and mass spectrometer. Additionally, the spacecraft will carry the Lunar Trailblazer small satellite, which will be deployed to map water deposits on the Moon to help NASA identify future landing sites for Artemis missions. Intuitive Machines has designed IM-2 to fly a more direct route to the Moon than some other missions, aiming to land just a week after launch.

Nokia is also mentioned in connection with the IM-2 mission, though the specific nature of their involvement is not fully public. Their participation likely relates to communications technology being tested on the lunar surface.

Future CLPS Missions and the Broader Lunar Exploration Strategy

Beyond the Blue Ghost and IM-2 missions, NASA has planned additional CLPS missions for 2025 and beyond. These include deliveries by companies such as Astrobotic, which experienced an anomaly with their Peregrine Mission One that prevented a lunar landing despite collecting data in transit.

Future CLPS flights will continue to target diverse regions of the Moon, including the near side, far side, and South Pole regions. Each area offers unique characteristics that inform the specific investigations and exploration objectives. This comprehensive approach ensures a thorough understanding of the lunar environment in preparation for human exploration.

The CLPS initiative plays a crucial role in NASA's broader Artemis campaign, which aims to return humans to the Moon and eventually send crewed missions to Mars. These robotic deliveries perform science experiments, test technologies, and demonstrate capabilities on and around the Moon to help NASA explore in advance of astronaut missions. The commercial approach also fosters a growing lunar economy both on and off Earth.

The Commercial Space Exploration Model

NASA's CLPS initiative represents a significant shift in how the agency approaches space exploration. Rather than building and operating its own landers, NASA now contracts with private companies to deliver its payloads to the Moon. This model has several advantages, including cost reduction, increased mission frequency, and the development of a sustainable commercial lunar industry.

The program operates by allowing companies to bid on contracts for lunar transport missions. This competitive approach encourages innovation and efficiency while distributing NASA's investment across multiple companies and technological approaches. The success of this model could significantly influence how space agencies around the world conduct future planetary exploration.

Michael Johansen, Flight Demonstrations Lead for NASA's Game Changing Development program, highlighted the unique value of these missions: "Replicating the Moon's harsh environment on Earth is a significant challenge because of extreme temperatures, low gravity, radiation, and dusty surface. The CLPS initiative provides unprecedented access to the lunar surface, allowing us to demonstrate technologies in the exact conditions they were designed for. Missions like Blue Ghost Mission 1 are a true game changer for NASA technology advancement and demonstration.

NASA's robotic missions planned for 2025 represent a robust lunar exploration program built on commercial partnerships through the CLPS initiative. With Firefly Aerospace's Blue Ghost mission set to land in March 2025 and Intuitive Machines' IM-2 mission targeting the lunar south pole in February, these missions will provide valuable scientific data and technological demonstrations that directly support NASA's Artemis program.

The $2.6 billion CLPS contract framework through 2028 ensures a sustained cadence of about two missions per year, allowing NASA to advance lunar science while simultaneously fostering a commercial lunar economy. These robotic precursors are essential for understanding the lunar environment, identifying resources, and testing technologies before human astronauts return to the Moon.

As 2025 unfolds, these missions will not only expand our scientific knowledge about Earth's nearest neighbor but also demonstrate the viability of a new commercial approach to space exploration that could become the template for future planetary missions beyond the Moon. Through these innovative partnerships, NASA is effectively leveraging private sector capabilities to achieve ambitious scientific goals while preparing for the next giant leap in human space exploration.

Influence of Private Equity and Global Finance Organizations

Private equity-backed venture capital investors are increasingly active in space start-up financing. These firms are, in many cases, started and run by former NASA professionals, university research lab-affiliated investors, or more traditional start-up investors diversifying into new markets.

They are all motivated by the growth of the commercial space industry, the existence of which they frequently promote, so as to support the virtuous cycle, they need to achieve a >10x return on investment. While the organic growth of the space industry is indeed enormous, they largely rely on or hope for a strong anchor customer such as NASA, the Defense Department, or international space agencies to reduce risk and secure long-term contracts.

Why It Matters: A Rich, Complex Web of Arrangements

Astute readers will recognize the remarkable variety of procurements and procurement mechanisms among the many listed projects. Few federal agencies have the range of vendors, timelines, and constraints that NASA functions within. NASA lore is full of stories of center leadership sent to Washington, D.C., to explain topics such as orbital dynamics to Congress to show why certain things must be done in a certain way.

Story Time Part 3: Government Shutdown 2013

In 2013, the government shut down for about three weeks, and I saw a really interesting feature of the way NASA is structured. JPL is not a civil service center; it is a contractor. So when the government shuts down, at least for a little while, the contractors stay open while the government centers are closed. These three weeks coincided with a proposal development period for an Earth observing mission opportunity. When the government shut down, our competition at the civil service centers had to stop working, but we did not, and we got three extra weeks of time and ultimately won the project. I thought that was pretty unfair, but it is what it is. I would later learn in the corporate world about the propensity for protest actions after a selection, as we have talked about in this book, but that did not happen in the 2013 case.

CHAPTER 4

How It Might Be

In this section, we will explore a series of different future scenarios for NASA.

The Status Quo: Steady as She Goes

Here we explore a future where NASA maintains its current course, focusing on lunar exploration, Mars missions, and incremental technological advancements.

NASA's goal was still to return people to the moon via the Artemis program in the year 2026 as the presidential administration changed in early 2025. There is usually turmoil and change as the administration turns over. Unique this time is the influence of Elon Musk on the administration and the reliance on his company for most U.S. government space launch. The Artemis program that was started during the first Trump administration already issued contracts to develop multiple lunar landers and space launch vehicles. It looks like blue origin will have an orbital vehicle in time to be competitive with SpaceX. Jeff Bezos and Amazon are ingratiating themselves with the Trump family to an extent that would be transparent influence buying under any previous administration, including Amazon paying first lady Melania Trump $40 million for the rights to make a biographic film about her on Amazon.

So, like so many other subjects in this book it is hard to speculate what contracting rules will actually be enforced in the next few years. Elon Musk himself is also making many public statements about how we should skip the moon and go straight to Mars. However, the Artemis programs contracts have been issued across the government and across the United States in many Senate districts and those representatives will not allow a major change in direction easily. If theoretically the administration decided to skip the moon and go to Mars, much of the work done by companies other than SpaceX would be hard to apply to the new destination. Traditionally, U.S. space exploration goals have been very hard to change, specifically because of the distribution of aerospace contractor work across many jurisdictions and congressional districts. At the same time, this administration is playing a lot of public debate just for TV cameras without apparent serious thought about implementation or actual policy in the traditional sense.

If we are to assume that there is not going to be a major policy change from the exploration goals of Artemis, then the business and contractual arrangements currently existing would probably persist. Elon Musk has made no secret of his wish to take over the entire program but seems clear at the time of this writing in June 2025 that this will not be the outcome. Further, the nominated administrator was rejected likely due to his proximity to Musk (the same reason for his original nomination in this chaotic administration) and another candidate has not been identified, confirmed, nor has anyone taken any acting control over NASA itself.

A Commercial Renaissance: NASA as a Partner

If we imagine that the incoming mass administrator ultimately severs all ties with the traditional aerospace industrial complex, then we can start to speculate about how current exploration goals would be restructured. The genius of early SpaceX was that the bar was set so low for traditional aerospace company performance that a rocket built in-house without extensive webs of subcontractors could come in under cost enough to make a reasonable profit and actually function. SpaceX has grown significantly in the 25 years since and currently holds many contracts with the federal government; some competitively won and some forced by litigation, as is the case with many national security launches.

Given the complexity of space hardware it's hard to imagine that something like the traditional supplier and distributor web does not emerge again as even SpaceX is starting to procure some of its parts from third parties. We can imagine a scenario where Boeing is completely excluded from competition—perhaps appropriately due to repeated, consecutive major failures of engineering management—but likely without the kind of procedural steps that would've occurred under any previous adminis-tration. We can also imagine SpaceX creating a deep space communica-tion system and forcing the administration to abandon reliance on the deep space network and TDRSS (the existing NASA near-Earth network) as seems eerily possible with Starlink.

This scenario harkens back to the early days of the postwar aerospace industry. At that time there were few conflicts of interest restrictions, and according to contemporary writers, officials awarded contracts to their friends at least partially out of a shared sense of duty need to get the job done as fast as possible. Obviously, that is an appealing perspective in hindsight and none of the restrictions put in place really made it pos-sible to deal in that way again. It's hard to compare the two approaches whether legacy airspace cost plus "complications" versus a U.S. govern-ment beholden to one billionaire with a space company. The only thing we can be sure about this while we gnash our teeth and spin our wheels, our adversaries make progress.

A Global Space Agency:
Collaboration Beyond Borders

Envisions a future where NASA becomes part of a larger, cooperative international space organization, sharing resources and expertise.

Thinking more broadly and perhaps further into the future, one might imagine a global space agency free of the partnering restrictions faced by NASA against working directly with China. An interesting example of international participation currently exists in the ESA, which follows a curious inversion of the system in the United States. The United States' one federal space agency spends money collected from all taxpayers on missions dictated by the executive branch. There is no relationship between the amount of money a certain state received for a space project from NASA to the amount of income tax paid by the citizens of that state. In fact the distribution of the initial NASA centers in the 1960s was overly political with only minor attention paid to even the practical-ities of space exploration. For example, the astronaut program is based in Texas while the astronauts fly out of Florida. There is no operational or technical reason for that; in fact, it would probably be easier if they were in the same place. However, at least Kennedy Space Center is in Florida where vehicles can launch to the east over the ocean sparing populated areas from damage in the event of a large failure.

In Europe, the member states of the ESA, which is most of them, pay into a common fund with the expectation that certain amounts of work will be distributed back to them roughly in proportion to what they put in. This arrangement in Europe works well given the lack of a unified federal system across the continent although it does increase the bureaucracy, and has led to criticisms that funding is used domestically to prop up companies without a justifiably large market.

India offers an interesting approach different from both in that it has distributed space centers like the USA except they are split up not by political affiliation but by function. For example, there is one space center for agriculture, one for environmental protection, one for military, and so on. Other nations such as Japan and Korea, being much smaller, following more NASA-like distribution of effort.

Many space missions have international components, particularly the large science investigations. We have not yet seen a truly global space effort largely because of lingering geopolitical disputes and because there is a protectionist nature of space funding given the large amounts of money involved and the domestic nature of most large aerospace contractors. A truly global effort would require one of two major changes that seem unlikely in the foreseeable future, one being the release of all geopolitical tensions allowing trust between nations with each other's advanced technology or a willingness of nations to either trust or disregard the notion of equal distribution of funding in favor of a larger goal. So far the geopolitical competitive and economic forces have led to rapid space exploration efforts in the 20th and 21st centuries. One can only imagine what humanity is capable of were we to work together, although that is not unique to space exploration.

The Return of the Space Race

This section analyzes a potential scenario where geopolitical tensions with countries like China or Russia ignite a new competitive drive, akin to the Cold War-era space race.

A tempting vision involves a repeat of the 1960s space race and some such as the previous administrator would argue that we are already in another space race with China. Even what is released publicly about China's goals on the moon shows an approach patterned closely after the Apollo programs missions Apollo 1 through 10, which built on each other, demonstrating discreet capabilities before using them all at once in Apollo 11 to actually land on the moon. Depending on how you break it up, China is somewhere between Apollo 8 and 9 although they have added the step of putting our communication system on the far side of the moon for reasons the author can only speculate about. I would argue that this is a repeat of the space race although only one participant is treating it as such.

Curiously and perhaps unexpectedly, the original foe of the United States in space, Russia has allowed it or deliberately enabled its space industry to become barely functional and has had its assets and value stripped by oligarchs and probably housed in European yachts and art. The Russian space program remains capable of transport to and from the ISS but not much else. It is not out of the realm of possibility that soon only SpaceX among the entire world is capable of delivering vehicles, and thus astronauts, to the space station should the Russian space program deteriorate further.

Should the United States accept that it is in a space race with China, precedent would indicate a relaxation of contractual procedures in favor of a rapid approach. However, that has partially already happened given the current administration's circumvention of procedure and account-ability in the contracting process. Still, it's not clear that even should all approaches move forward as fast as possible, that the United States could match the Chinese capability in space at the speed of progress with which the latter is moving.

Interstellar Ambitions:
Pushing Beyond the Solar System

Details the technologies and missions that could take NASA beyond our solar system, inspired by concepts such as solar sails and interstellar probes (note, the author has directly led research projects in these areas).

One possible extremely ambitious mission that could involve many nations is a robotic interstellar mission. We have already explored interstellar space to some degree with the Voyager spacecraft. They left the solar system around 2014 but they were not designed to function long at that extreme distance and are running out of power. Following up on those missions would be a worthy goal for any space agency but a significant effort would require participation from multiple nations. The reasons for this would include numerous technology advances particularly in the energy storage and communications areas. NASA has done some very early exploratory work in this area building on the New Horizons mission, which itself built on the Voyager missions themselves. A mission like this would be scientific in nature and would probably involve multiple NASA centers working in partnership and a global science team. Global science teams are built with different types of contracts between NASA and U.S.-based research centers, which then make agreements with foreign universities. It is not unheard of for NASA to send money to foreign universities but it is usually preferable to avoid that if possible.

The Apollo program, by multiple economic studies actually was a net positive financial investment. This is because it required the creation of many technologies that would come to underpin the economy today such as many computers, transistors, software development, and many technologies for life support that went on to be part of modern medical equipment. This is one of the harder cases to make to the American public to the point where several historians of this subject have said that it's not worth trying but it's still worth mentioning here for you, the reader. Choosing an exceptionally ambitious goal such as an interstellar mission would likely result in the creation of a wide range of currently unimaginable technologies that would probably flow down to commercial uses, similar to Apollo.

A Focus on Earth: Turning Inward

Explores the possibility of NASA redirecting its efforts toward Earth-focused challenges such as climate monitoring and disaster management.

The opposite of an interstellar focus would be a focus on the Earth system itself. There are hundreds of Earth-orbiting and Earth-observing satellites in operation today. These are operated by most nations that have a space program as launching into space and looking down on the Earth is one of the earlier and "easier" projects to attempt. It is also among the easier projects to sell to internal domestic stakeholders of any nation as having a source of earth system data controlled by your nation is preferable to always trusting international sources even if you are duplicating the technical effort of others. This also leads to the development of domestic talent. Earth observation missions also lead to one of the more lucrative space business models: the imagery and weather prediction markets.

Many billions of dollars are spent every year on Earth observation imagery and climate and weather modeling. The current administration is making an effort to dismantle parts of the National Oceanographic Administration presumably to allow the privatization of some of its efforts. It remains to be seen whether this will succeed or be stopped or reversed by the courts, but in principle that could create a business opportunity for a future satellite operator.

The Moon as a Gateway: Lunar First

Delves into the potential of lunar bases as a stepping stone for deeper space exploration and their role in scientific discovery.

Part of the current Artemis plan involves a so-called gateway space station orbiting the moon. The rationale for this is that by operating a space station much farther away than the current one we will develop the capabilities necessary to send people to further destination such as Mars. In reality, the people who want to currently operate the international space station are terrified that they will not have a space station to operate under the new Artemis plan. So they have via various means inserted a space station around the moon as part of the program. If that space station remains part of the plan, and I suspect it will not, it will be an enormous financial drain with limited practical uses. It's not that it will never make sense to have a lunar space station but that it is such an enormous effort that it would not be practical to operate that while also trying to land people on the moon or send them to Mars. The most useful insight from this possibility is simply that of the influence of the current contractors who operate the space station basically trying to force another space station into whatever plan comes next.

Mars and Beyond: A Human Presence on Other Worlds

Imagines a future where Mars colonization becomes a centerpiece of NASA's mission, alongside plans for human exploration of other celestial bodies.

Multiple administrations have stated that sending humans to Mars is part of their goals. As long ago as the early 1970s, NASA worked on mission architecture concepts to send humans to Mars (with the remaining Saturn V rockets from Apollo). In modern times, this at least goes back to the early 2010s. I distinctly remember a moment in 2012 when I was at JPL and the NASA twitter account posted a message about taking steps to Mars. That was the first time in my career with NASA that such a goal was stated. I looked around and thought "wait, what?" As there was no messaging internally about this.

Politicians are notorious for not understanding the challenges of space exploration, especially the magnitude of the difference between sending people to the moon and sending people to Mars. An early space industry luminary, Gentry Lee, was sent to congress in the 1970s and retold a story about explaining why we can only go to Mars every few years—using the analogy of a train that only leaves every 18 months due to the orbital dynamics involved.

I suspect this is why so many administration plans include human Mars visits, and the latest version is no different. The day before this paragraph was written, SpaceX lost a second starship vehicle during a test flight. We are a long way from sending that vehicle to the moon, let alone Mars. With Boeing's challenges even getting to the space station, we are not going anywhere fast that way either.

Radical Reorganization: NASA 2.0

Considers dramatic shifts in NASA's structure, including privatization, decentralization, or a complete overhaul of its mission priorities.

On Monday, March 10, 2025, NASA announced it was terminating several offices. This will include several offices focused on diversity and inclusion, which is at least consistent with the administrative guidance, but it is also terminating the position of the chief scientist of NASA. Earlier this week there were reports that NASA is also going to suffer a 50 percent budget cut to its science division. Many advocacy organizations have stood up to oppose this but at the time of this writing it is unclear what the outcome will be. Congressional budget negotiation is a complicated process. However, in this case, the Republican-led Congress has completely accepted the Trump administration actions with little protest.

In a normal budget process the executive branch request might be aggressive in order to end up halfway there after negotiation, but it's not clear there will be the necessary pushback this time. Even if met in the middle at a 25 percent budget cut it would have devastating effects for the space science community. Even stranger, the support of NASA is one of the only things remotely consistent from all of this administration's messaging since before the 2024 election. It's hard to see, even cynically, a good reason for these cuts because it is a relatively small amount of money to save and many of the proposed cuts are missions with over 90 percent sunk costs.

Cynically, one can imagine a justification for cutting government projects and services so that a private company connected to the administration can replace the services (the typical privatization argument). However, there is no private incentive to perform these science missions that would be so utterly ruined by a 50 percent budget cut. There are no private entities capable of doing these projects. Maybe the justification is that some private entity will spring up to meet this demand. But that strikes me as hopelessly naïve. The "privatization at all costs team" cannot possibly be so naïve themselves that they think someone will find a profit motive here, can they?

Whatever the reason, cutting the NASA budget by 50 percent would not only make existing projects impossible to complete but it would also probably doom a dozen active spacecraft around the solar system. This gets to a larger question of how do you manage multiple year-long and even decade-long projects in a four-year administrative priority cycle that is baked into the U.S. constitution. So that is on the author's mind today as I sat down to write this section about reorganizing NASA.

Thinking a bit further, there are some rational approaches to reorganizing NASA that could be done at some point. NASA distribution around the country was never based on anything logical or practical but rather the appeasement of different senators in the 1960s. The work distributed to the centers likewise is only logically connected because of the facilities built up nationwide. So to move or close a center would be a major undertaking because the capabilities there would likely have to be reproduce elsewhere. Although the argument could be made that those are the kinds of services that are private entity could offer at a lower cost to the tax fair. For example, there are many different kinds of laboratories and test facilities at NASA centers that by now in 2025 could be offered on a private basis, even if they could not be supported in that sense back when they were built in the 1960s and 1970s.

But this would require a thorough and careful evaluation of existing facilities and projects and demands, which is clearly not happening at the moment at least at the federal level when the focus is on firing as many people as possible. Still, that could be a rational approach to take in the future if a serious attempt at this kind of reorganization was of interest. I have personally seen the dynamics between NASA centers actively prevent things from happening where one NASA center is so insistent on getting a piece of a project that it requires the inclusion of a space system or technology that does not even make sense for the mission. So it certainly is common that centers can put their own self-preservation ahead of even the ultimate success of missions. I don't think this ends up happening all the way to the launchpad (although the gateway space station around the moon is an example of this and hopefully will not happen.) So some effort and energy could be saved with a different approach than self-preservation at all costs for the centers.

As mentioned elsewhere, other nations have different strategies for building and distributing their space centers. I have always been partial to the Indian system where the centers are distributed around the country on a functional or subject matter basis instead of a political one.

The author finds it hard to think beyond the immediate threatened cuts to the science program however and is forced to reevaluate something he had concluded over the years. I had thought that the NASA space science budget was relatively safe because it was never enough money, especially compared to the human flight program, to be worth fighting over. That budget for the science program had always been roughly 15 to 20 percent of the overall NASA budget and the major aerospace contractor seemed content to receive 80 or so percent for their human programs. The planetary science program started in the 1960s as efforts were necessary to study the surface of the moon before Apollo 11 would land there. NASA built from there to send probes to all the planets of the solar system and land on several of them. It's one of the most amazing achievements in human history as far as the author is concerned.

Unknown Unknowns

It's hard to say exactly how NASA should be structured because it's not even clear what the mission of NASA actually is anymore. NASA has been most effective historically in response to major events, such as the Soviet Union Sputnik event and the race to the moon. Another example would be the ISS, which was largely a reaction to the fall of the Soviet Union and the need to give thousands of engineers and scientists something productive to do on a global level so they would not resort to seeking employment in destructive applications of their abilities. In the middle of that was the shuttle program, which was originally designed to be the U.S. delivery truck to LEO. Planetary exploration, A by-product of the Apollo program was the beginning of what would become 50 years of planetary exploration, which I would argue is one of the most successful things NASA ever did.

Sometimes people ask me what I would do if I was in charge of NASA and my answer depends on how long they have. The person in charge of NASA is called the administrator and that title is true in every sense of the word in that the role is to administer someone else's goal. That person is, of course, the President of the United States, who directs the ultimate goals of Nasa in response to influence and pressure from many different directions. So fundamentally what I would do if I was the president regarding space would be heavily based on what NASA has shown itself to be effective at in the past. In my opinion, that is setting ambitious goals without a clear commercial benefit and challenging industry to engineer solutions. NASA itself, of course, operates many incredible facilities, but in my opinion, they should be used for technical challenges that have not yet shown a commercial purpose.

Unfortunately, at least since the year 2000 one level above policy has become the issue, by which I am referring to the actual structure of the U.S. government up to the constitution. Changing leadership every four years has turned out to be very difficult for making long-term space exploration plans that are not urgent such as Apollo. And even Apollo probably only came to fruition because Kennedy was assassinated and there was still enough bipartisan respect for legacy at that time. Nowadays, every administration changes the space program and it's very difficult to make plans that take longer than four to eight years, let alone sustaining something permanent someday like a Moon base or a Mars program.

Ignoring that for the moment, though, if I was the president, I would set a goal of a four-year-long Moon excursion. That's long enough that it would require the development of entirely new technologies, but not permanent, which as I mentioned would probably strain the ability of the U.S. government to maintain a singular vision. The Artemis program, which may well be canceled within a month of the writing of this paragraph, is a largely symbolic return to the Moon of a single short-term mission that arguably is an example of a lack of imagination more than anything else. Well, a lack of imagination and the overwhelming influence of the legacy aerospace contractors who want to get paid again to use bunch of the same technology as 50 years ago to do something we've already done.

Meanwhile, China is effectively moving toward a human Moon landing mission following essentially the same steps that the United States did in the 1960s with Apollo 1 through 10. I don't think there is sufficient discussion at the national level about what NASA's role actually is. The way things are currently going China will reach the Moon before the United States does, which will either be an embarrassment to the United States or the opposite depending on how we set our goals. For example, if we had an actual funded program of going to Mars with people, then it wouldn't matter if China got to the Moon first. However, that is a bit naïve as it ignores the strategic and military value that the Moon potentially offers. Once again, the United States is limited by its four-year planning horizon let alone the fact that the legacy aerospace industry has so captured the government that even though it has repeatedly failed to stay on target and schedule, Boeing still dominates the official human landing program on the Moon.

Getting back to the actual job of NASA, I would argue that it is to project the most positive virtues of the United States as far across the solar system as humanly possible. I often reflect on the mid to late 1960s, during which the United States was both getting more and more bogged down in Vietnam, as well as getting closer and closer to the moon. In fact, President Johnson had many days where he would go from a meeting about Apollo to a meeting about Vietnam, and I am simply boggled by the comparison. Putting aside that seeming hypocritical American exceptionalism, I still think the best value for NASA is to represent the best qualities of what makes America unique, or at least what once did. In doing so, it can also create extraordinary economic value as it did during Apollo by setting audacious technology and engineering goals that, once derisked by flight, find extensive commercial applications.

Unfortunately, the legacy aerospace industry showed that it was highly effective in minimizing ambition in order to maximize sales of existing equipment and services. As of this writing, SpaceX, which the entire U.S. government relies on for space access, is showing cracks in its leadership and reliability and no small part by the chaotic behavior of its president Elon Musk. Unfortunately, as of early 2025, his personal conduct rampaging across the federal government is grounds for contract termination across his company should a levelheaded arbiter of conflict of interest law take the most casual glance.

The *idea* of NASA is too important to the future of American technology to depend on the current views of specific individuals, no matter how well known and accomplished in whatever their fields are. It would be ideal if a small panel of knowledgeable experts, without any financial interest in the results of their recommendations, could chart a course for "Starship NASA." Dare I say the course should "boldly go" in search of "potentially useful scientific objectives," thereby continuing to seed our economies with the technologies required to accomplish those scientific missions.

Why It Matters: Possible Futures Collapsed

In mid-August 2025, the acting NASA administrator announced that NASA will stop performing earth science research and focus entirely on human transportation. This is not exactly a future that people within NASA were expecting, as science has been a core part of NASA since the beginning of the agency. It appears that the Trump administration considers NASA to be a human transportation agency, a view supported by the fact that the acting administrator is also the acting administrator of the Federal Aviation Administration. The preceding possible futures were all written between February and August 2025, before this major announcement was made. The impact of the announcement is unclear because the administrator does not have the legal authority to do that, but it underscores the possibility of rapid and unpredicted change in NASA priorities as administrations change.

Story Time Part 4: Won a Big Phase 2 in My Underwear

Among the most meaningful personal/professional events was a project that I started in 2012 to design a mission to measure the interior of caves on the moon. The multiple phases of this project cross my departure from JPL in 2014 due to my wife's career in surgery. I won the first phase while supported by the entire JPL organization and I won the second phase while writing the proposal in my underwear alone in Maryland. That launched my confidence that I could contribute meaningfully to Space exploration independently, which I continue to do to this day, including the writing of this book.

Story Time Part 5: "Fucking Moron"

Among my consulting engagements was a very rewarding three-year proposal management role at Johns Hopkins University Applied Physics Laboratory (APL) from 2016 to 2019. I was a proposal manager for several missions, one of which is launching in the fall of 2025 during the manuscript review period of this book. Part of that work involves reviewing complex "Request for Proposal" documents from NASA and structuring a response that is both scientifically compelling and compliant with the rules. At one point, during a presentation to senior leadership of the Lab, the principal investigator, upon hearing my analysis of the requirements, shouted loudly that I was a "fucking moron."

To say at least this was a surprise, as was the total lack of any response from anyone in the room, including people senior to him. I've been called a lot of things by a lot of people, but never or something quite like that in that situation. There was probably no response from the organization because I was a consultant, not an employee, but that does not mean it was constructive or professional obviously. I later addressed this privately with him, and he ultimately agreed that I was right in my interpretation, and he was wrong to express himself in that way. Unfortunately, that kind of emotional lack of control is not uncommon. That particular proposal was ultimately unsuccessful, but not because of my interpretation of the rules and my engagement at APL ended in 2019 when the government shut down again.

CHAPTER 5

Navigating NASA's Next-Decade Business Challenges

In the coming decade, doing business with NASA will require grappling with a rapidly changing landscape. As we conclude, five major challenges stand out as critical for NASA and its partners. These challenges—ranging from global competition to public perception and market dynamics—will shape strategic decisions and partnerships. In the following sections, we analyze each challenge in turn, providing a business-focused perspective supported by recent data and expert insights.

The Rise of China

China's ascent in space is a defining strategic challenge for NASA. Beijing has articulated an ambitious long-term vision—effectively a **100-year space plan**—aimed at establishing China as the world's leading space power by mid-century. In late 2024, Chinese officials unveiled a comprehensive 2024–2050 space exploration roadmap with one goal: *"to make China a world leader in space by 2050."* This plan lays out phased milestones, including crewed Moon landings by 2030 and the construction of an international lunar research station in the early 2030s. Such long-range planning highlights China's capacity for sustained commitment. As one analyst observed, the new plan is a clear *"sign that they're committed"* to space for the long term, despite economic uncertainties. In contrast to NASA's budget cycles and shifting political winds, China's one-party system affords continuity with **limited offramps**—once a program is approved at high levels, it is likely to persist for decades.

For NASA's business partners, China's rise presents both competitive and collaborative implications. Chinese state-backed industries are rapidly advancing satellite networks, human spaceflight, and deep-space exploration, often with generous funding and nationalistic fervor. More than **100 orbital launches** were planned by China in 2023 alone, signaling a high operational tempo that rivals U.S. activity. Beijing's long-term approach, sometimes described as a marathon, means Chinese space enterprises can afford to play the long game. They are courting international partners through initiatives like a proposed lunar research station, potentially drawing countries and markets away from U.S.-led projects. The challenge for NASA and American aerospace firms will be maintaining technological and economic leadership in this environment. It will require innovation and agility to match China's **capacity for long-term investment**. NASA's commercial partners, in particular, will need strategies to remain competitive on cost and capability, lest China's commitment erode the U.S. edge in the global space economy. As one expert put it, China's steady fulfillment of its space objectives—it has been *"very successful at meeting its own goals and timelines"*—underscores that this competition is structural, not easily deterred by momentary setbacks.

American Apathy

A less tangible but equally serious challenge is domestic apathy toward space endeavors. Even as NASA pursues ambitious programs such as Artemis (returning astronauts to the Moon) and Mars exploration, public interest and awareness lag. Recent polling data reveals a striking **disconnect between NASA's goals and public priorities**. In a 2023 Pew Research Center survey, only **12 percent of Americans** said that sending astronauts to the Moon should be a top NASA priority, and a mere **11 percent** felt the same about crewed Mars exploration. By contrast, much larger shares of the public want NASA to focus on near-Earth concerns—for example, 60 percent rated monitoring asteroids for Earth impact as a top priority, and 50 percent prioritized climate science from space. This misalignment suggests that NASA's high-profile human exploration missions are not capturing broad public enthusiasm. For businesses, this **apathy** translates into a risk factor: lack of public interest can lead to fragile political support and funding vulnerability for NASA programs.

Indeed, signs of wavering support are evident in budget attitudes. A recent Marquette Law School poll found that **63 percent of Americans support cutting NASA's budget** as a way to reduce the federal deficit.[39] NASA's funding, roughly half a percent of federal spending, is often misunderstood by the public—and when belt-tightening becomes a priority, space expenditures can become an easy target. The business community must recognize that NASA's future projects (and the contracts they generate) will depend on sustained advocacy and clear demonstration of value to the American public. If voters and lawmakers view missions to the Moon or Mars as nice-to-have rather than need-to-have, those projects could face delays or cancelation, directly impacting contractors and suppliers. Conversely, reframing NASA's work in terms of tangible benefits—such as economic growth, technological innovation, and national prestige—will be crucial. The agency may need to **recalibrate its communication strategy** to bridge the gap. As one analysis noted, the lack of public enthusiasm for lunar missions could make it harder to *"maintain political and financial support for the Artemis program,"* forcing NASA to work harder to justify its investments. For businesses, partnering with NASA will not just be about meeting technical requirements; it will also entail helping to tell a compelling story of why these missions matter to taxpayers and the nation's future.

European Doubt

International partnerships have long been a cornerstone of NASA's missions, but recent developments threaten to erode allies' trust. A case in point is the **Rosalind Franklin Mars rover** (part of the European-led ExoMars mission). After global events derailed the rover's 2022 launch, Europe looked to NASA and the United States for help in delivering the rover to Mars. However, proposed U.S. budget cuts in 2025 targeted NASA's support for this mission, effectively backing out of a prior commitment. The rover's launch vehicle and descent stage were to be provided by NASA; without them, ESA cannot proceed unless it finds an alternative heavy-lift launcher. While no final decision has been made (Congress is reviewing the budget), the mere prospect of a U.S. withdrawal has sent shockwaves through the transatlantic space community. Such moves have **diplomatic costs**. European leaders have openly warned that if Washington cancels its support now—especially after a similar NASA pull-out from ExoMars in 2012—it *"would cement the perception that U.S. commitments last no longer than a presidential term."* In other words, Europe is beginning to doubt whether NASA will be a reliable partner beyond the next election cycle.

The erosion of trust has concrete business implications. Major international projects often span decades (space telescopes, lunar gateways, Mars sample return, etc.), and partners need confidence that technical and financial contributions will endure. A **reputation for unpredictability** could cost NASA future collaborations or force allies to seek more self-reliance. European officials are already discussing "sovereignty" in space endeavors—investing in domestic capabilities to reduce reliance on U.S. hardware and funding. ESA is weighing closer ties with alternative partners (Japan, India, and even exploring cooperation with China in extremis) to ensure that *"no single foreign veto can stall"* a flagship program again. For NASA contractors, this trend might mean fewer joint missions to bid on or more competition from European firms if Europe internalizes work that might have gone to U.S. suppliers. Additionally, losing international projects can shrink the overall pie of mission opportunities. The **"permanent dent in Washington's reputational capital"** from a high-profile withdrawal may take years to mend. To mitigate European doubt, NASA leadership and U.S. industry will need to emphasize consistency and perhaps new models of partnership that provide allies greater guarantees. Demonstrating commitment—for example, by backing cooperative programs through multiyear legislation or building in fail-safes against abrupt cancelation—could help restore confidence and keep transatlantic ventures attractive for all parties involved.

Scams and Bad Actors

Not all challenges are external; some arise from within the aerospace ecosystem. As the space sector booms, **fraudulent and disingenuous actors** pose a growing risk, eroding trust in science and technology endeavors.

NASA's projects, with their technical complexity and enormous budgets, have unfortunately attracted occasional bad actors in the supply chain. History has shown that a single unscrupulous supplier can wreak havoc. In one egregious case, a metals manufacturer falsified critical test results for years, supplying substandard aluminum that led to the failure of two NASA satellite missions—a disaster that cost the agency over **$700 million.**[40] The investigation revealed that the fraud spanned 19 years and hundreds of contracts. As NASA's Launch Services director summed up, "*when testing results are altered and certifications provided falsely, missions fail,*" leading to years of work lost. The NASA Inspector General's office continues to uncover similar issues: from counterfeit parts to forged safety documents. A recent OIG report highlighted that **substandard components** and fake compliance certifications can "*lead to mission failures, launch delays, increased costs, and safety risks.*" For businesses contracting with NASA, these incidents serve as cautionary tales. They underscore the importance of rigorous quality control and ethics—not only to avoid legal consequences but also to protect the collective reputation of NASA's industrial base. A high-profile failure caused by one contractor's misconduct can tarnish many vendors by association, prompting more invasive oversight and reducing NASA's willingness to engage new suppliers.

Beyond the technical supply chain, **frauds in the commercial space sector** threaten investor and public confidence. The past few years have seen not only a surge of capital into space start-ups but also a few headline-grabbing scandals. In 2021, for example, the SEC charged a space technology company (Momentus Inc.) and its SPAC sponsor with securities fraud, alleging that they misled investors about the success of a propulsion technology test and downplayed national security red flags.[41] The company had claimed a successful in-space demonstration when in fact the test failed to achieve its primary objectives. Such deception not only resulted in financial penalties but also sent a warning to the whole industry. Inflated claims, hype without substance, or outright scams (as seen in other tech domains) can make governments and investors more skeptical about legitimate aerospace ventures. From a business standpoint, **due diligence** and transparency are paramount. NASA and its partners will likely institute even stricter vetting of contractors' technical claims and financial health. Companies that cut corners or overpromise recklessly may find themselves blacklisted, as NASA moves to protect its missions and taxpayer dollars. Conversely, firms that commit to strong compliance cultures can differentiate themselves. The bottom line is that trust—among the public, investors, and NASA itself—is a precious currency. Every fraudulent actor in the space arena devalues that currency, making it harder for the rest to do business. Protecting the integrity of the field will be an ongoing challenge as the sector grows.

Crony Capture

A final challenge is the potential **overreliance on a single private actor**—a scenario that could lead to a quasi-monopoly or "crony capture" of NASA's critical programs. In recent years, SpaceX in particular has become indispensable to U.S. space efforts. The company's reliability and cost-effective launch services have not only benefited NASA enormously but they also created vulnerability. By 2025, **more than half of all active satellites** in orbit had been launched by SpaceX rockets, and SpaceX was receiving billions in government contracts annually (about **$3.8 billion in 2024** alone). With successes like the Falcon 9 and Crew Dragon, SpaceX now carries astronauts, supplies the ISS, and is slated to land astronauts on the Moon via its Starship Human Landing System. The concern is that NASA's portfolio has, intentionally or not, become heavily tied to one contractor. If something were to go wrong—technically or politically—NASA's missions could face severe disruption. A U.S. Space Force official bluntly highlighted this risk: *"Heaven forbid we have a mishap with a Falcon 9 launch... that means it is grounded, right? And that means we could be without launch."* In other words, lacking redundant capabilities, a single-point failure in SpaceX's fleet might halt America's access to space. From a business continuity perspective, that is a serious single-source risk.

Moreover, reliance can morph into **monopolistic behavior** over time. SpaceX's dominant market position has few precedents in space history outside of nation-state programs. There are already allegations from industry competitors that SpaceX leverages its clout to undercut or exclude rivals. For instance, other launch providers have claimed that SpaceX uses predatory pricing—offering satellite rideshare launches at below cost, subsidized by its government contracts—to capture market share and stifle emerging players. Some customers signing up with

SpaceX have found themselves agreeing to exclusivity clauses that prevent them from using alternative launch services. This kind of **market capture** raises concerns that innovation and supply diversity could suffer, especially if new entrants can't gain a foothold. The scenario draws parallels to the **post-Soviet Russian space industry**, where a single organization (Roscosmos) monopolized crewed launch services for nearly a decade. With NASA dependent on Soyuz spacecraft after 2011, Roscosmos dramatically increased prices—NASA's cost for an astronaut seat jumped from about $22 million in 2008 to $81 million by 2018 (a **372 percent increase**) as Russia capitalized on its monopoly.[42] At the same time, the lack of competition contributed to stagnation and complacency. The lesson is clear: if NASA becomes **overreliant on one company**, it risks not only paying more in the long run but also exposure to that company's internal challenges or strategic whims.

To address this challenge, NASA and policymakers are already taking action by encouraging competition. Initiatives like the Commercial Crew Program (which deliberately had two providers, SpaceX and Boeing) and the decision to fund a second Artemis lunar lander provider are steps to avoid a single point of failure. For businesses, the message is to stay competitive and seek niches where diversification is valued. It's also a caution to SpaceX itself—history shows that monopolistic dominance often invites government intervention or a push for alternatives (as seen with antitrust discussions around Starlink and launch services). **Crony capture** of NASA's agenda by any one actor could also breed political backlash, especially if concerns arise about undue influence or favoritism in contracting. A healthy space economy, much like any other market, thrives on multiple players, robust competition, and resilience through redundancy. Ensuring that SpaceX's success does not crowd out all others—and that NASA doesn't become captive to one corporate "crown jewel"—will be a delicate balancing act in the years ahead.

Sources: Recent reports and expert analyses were used to inform this conclusion, including data on public opinion, international partnerships, industry fraud cases, and market trends. These references underscore the multifaceted challenges NASA and its business partners must navigate as they forge the future of space exploration. By anticipating these challenges—and responding with strategic, collaborative solutions—the NASA enterprise can continue to thrive in a new era of opportunity and risk.

Why It Matters

NASA was founded in 1958 amid the intense geopolitical rivalry of the Cold War, serving as a key instrument to project American technological prowess and leadership on the global stage. The Soviet Union's launch of Sputnik in 1957 had jolted the United States, sparking fears of falling behind in both scientific innovation and military capability. In response, NASA became a symbol of American determination to lead in space exploration, culminating in the Apollo Moon landings, which were as much about demonstrating superiority as they were about scientific discovery.

Understanding this context is crucial for predicting NASA's future priorities, as historical patterns suggest that national security interests, global competition, and technological leadership will continue to influence its priorities and political direction. As emerging powers assert themselves in space, and as new domains such as lunar resources and power projection via Mars exploration gain strategic importance, NASA's objectives will likely reflect both scientific ambition and the enduring imperative to uphold American leadership.

Story Time Part 6: "I Accept Cash, Checks, and Gold Bullion"

Throughout 2012 to 2019 I was involved in my lunar cave mapping project on and off as proposal opportunities came along. In 2019, I had the opportunity to present the project to the administrator of Nasa on Capitol Hill during an event called Nasa day on the hill. Not a shy person, I more or less cornered the NASA administrator as he walked by and offered to present my project to him. He obliged, and after explaining it to him, he said it should be a program of record, which is government speak for an official project with funding. Without missing a beat I said, "Well I accept cash checks and gold bullion" and he gave me a funny look. Nothing further came a bit despite repeated attempts, but at least I tried.

References

1. "BBC News—Science & Nature: '7800721'." *BBC News*. n.d. http://news.bbc.co.uk/2/hi/science/nature/7800721.stm (accessed August 19, 2025).
2. "Commercial Orbital Transportation Services." *Wikipedia*, last modified n.d. https://en.wikipedia.org/wiki/Commercial_Orbital_Transportation_Services (accessed August 19, 2025).
3. "SpaceX Reusable Launch System Development Program." *Wikipedia*, last modified n.d. https://en.wikipedia.org/wiki/SpaceX_reusable_launch_system_development_program (accessed August 19, 2025).
4. "Test Flight of Antares Rocket Set for Wednesday Evening." *Spaceflight Now*. https://spaceflightnow.com/antares/demo/130416 preview/ (accessed August 19, 2025).
5. NASA. n.d. *Report No. 20170008895: NASA Commercial Orbital Transportation Services (COTS) Program*. NASA Technical Reports Server. https://ntrs.nasa.gov/api/citations/20170008895/downloads/20170008895.pdf (accessed August 19, 2025).
6. NASA. n.d. "New Report Analyzes Long History of NASA Support for Commercial Space." *NASA*. https://www.nasa.gov/organizations/otps/new-report-analyzes-long-history-of-nasa-support-for-commercial-space/ (accessed August 19, 2025).
7. NASA Office of Inspector General. June 13, 2013. *IG-13-016: Commercial Cargo: NASA's Management of Commercial Orbital Transportation Services and ISS Commercial Resupply Contracts*. https://oig.nasa.gov/wp-content/uploads/2024/02/IG-13-016.pdf (accessed August 19, 2025).
8. "NASA Awards Space Station Commercial Resupply Services Contracts to SpaceX and Orbital." *SpaceNews*. n.d. https://spacenews.com/nasa-awards-space-station-commercial-resupply-services-contracts-to-spacex-and-orbital/ (accessed August 19, 2025).
9. "Boeing and SpaceX Awarded Contracts to Fill the Void Left by NASA's Retired Space Shuttles." *AmericaSpace*. September 16, 2014. https://www.americaspace.com/2014/09/16/boeing-and-spacex-

awarded-contracts-to-fill-the-void-left-by-nasas-retired-space-shuttles/ (accessed August 19, 2025).

10. NASA. April 16, 2021. "As Artemis Moves Forward, NASA Picks SpaceX to Land Next Americans on Moon." *NASA.* https://www .nasa.gov/news-release/as-artemis-moves-forward-nasa-picks-spacex-to-land-next-americans-on-moon/ (accessed August 19, 2025).

11. NASA Office of Inspector General. October 10, 2018. *IG19001: NASA's Management of the Space Launch System Stages Contract.* https://oig.nasa.gov/wp-content/uploads/2024/02/IG-19-001.pdf (accessed August 19, 2025).

12. NASA. December 2, 2021. "NASA Selects Companies to Develop Commercial Destinations in Space." *NASA.* https://www.nasa. gov/news-release/nasa-selects-companies-to-develop-commercial-destinations-in-space/ (accessed August 19, 2025).

13. NASA. n.d. "Grants Policy and Compliance Team." *NASA.* https://www.nasa.gov/grants-policy-and-compliance-team/ (accessed August 19, 2025).

14. NASA Office of Inspector General. November 30, 2021. *IG22005: NASA's Management of the International Space Station and Efforts to Commercialize Low Earth Orbit.* https://oig.nasa.gov/wp-content/ uploads/2024/02/IG-22-005.pdf (accessed August 19, 2025).

15. NASA. n.d. "Current Space Act Agreements." *NASA.* https:// www.nasa.gov/partnerships/current-space-act-agreements/ (accessed August 19, 2025).

16. NASA. n.d. "SBIR/STTR Program." *NASA.* https://www.nasa.gov/ sbir_sttr/ (accessed August 19, 2025).

17. Kessler, J.L. October 2019. "Space Portal." *NASA.* https://www .nasa.gov/wp-content/uploads/2019/10/space_portal_jason_l._ kessler.pdf (accessed August 19, 2025).

18. Loura Hall. September 8, 2016. "NASA Awards $750K in Sample Return Robot Challenge for Autonomous Technology." *NASA.* https://www.nasa.gov/directorates/stmd/prizes-challenges-crowd sourcing-program/nasa-awards-750k-in-sample-return-robot-challenge-for-autonomous-technology/ (accessed August 19, 2025).

19. Clark, S. November 4, 2021. "Blue Origin Loses Lawsuit, Clearing Way for NASA to Move Forward with SpaceX Moon Lander."

Spaceflight Now. https://spaceflightnow.com/2021/11/04/blue-origin-loses-lawsuit-clearing-way-for-nasa-to-move-forward-with-spacex-moon-lander/ (accessed August 19, 2025).

20. "Sierra Nevada Protests NASA's CCtCAP Awards." *SpacePolicy Online*. September 26, 2014. https://spacepolicyonline.com/news/sierra-nevada-protests-nasas-cctcap-awards/ (accessed August 19, 2025).

21. "PlanetSpace Has Filed With the GAO a Protest to the Selection Decision of NASA under the ISS Commercial Resupply Services (CRS) Competition." *SpaceNews*. January 15, 2009. https://spacenews.com/planetspace-has-filed-with-the-gao-a-protest-to-the-selection-decision-of-nasa-under-the-iss-commercial-resupply-services-crs-competition/ (accessed August 19, 2025).

22. "SpaceX Files Protest of NASA's Lucy Launch Contract Awarded to ULA." *Spaceflight Now*. February 15, 2019. https://spaceflightnow.com/2019/02/15/spacex-files-protest-of-nasas-lucy-launch-contract-awarded-to-ula/ (accessed August 19, 2025).

23. U.S. Government Accountability Office. April 22, 2009. "B401016; B401016.2—PlanetSpace, Inc." *GAO*. https://www.gao.gov/products/b-401016 (accessed August 19, 2025).

24. "Spacehab Files Tort Claim for Losses on Space Shuttle Mission." *SpaceNews*. February 3, 2006. https://spacenews.com/spacehab-files-tort-claim-for-losses-on-space-shuttle-mission/ (accessed August 19, 2025).

25. "Boeing Protests $1.09 Billion GOESR Contract Award to Lockheed Martin." *Defense Daily*. December 17, 2008. https://www.defense-daily.com/boeing-protests-1-09-billion-goes-r-contract-award-to-lockheed-martin/uncategorized/ (accessed August 19, 2025).

26. NASA. n.d. "NASA Shares Orion Heat Shield Findings, Updates Artemis Moon Missions." *NASA*. https://www.nasa.gov/news-release/nasa-shares-orion-heat-shield-findings-updates-artemis-moon-missions/ (accessed August 19, 2025).

27. Fowler, S. August 2025. "After Recent Tests, China Appears Likely to Beat the United States Back to the Moon." *Ars Technica*. https://arstechnica.com/space/2025/08/after-recent-tests-china-appears-likely-to-beat-the-united-states-back-to-the-moon/ (accessed August 19, 2025).

28. NASA. n.d. "The Artemis Accords: Principles for Cooperation in the Civil Exploration and Use of the Moon, Mars, Comets, and Asteroids." *NASA.* https://www.nasa.gov/artemis-accords/ (accessed August 19, 2025).

29. NASA Office of Inspector General. October 5, 2023. *IG-24-003: NASA's Management of the Mars Sample Return Program.* https:// oig.nasa.gov/wp-content/uploads/2023/10/ig-24-003.pdf (accessed August 19, 2025).

30. Berger, E. July 17, 2020. "NASA's Inspector General Report Roasts Lockheed Martin for Orion Fees." *Ars Technica.* https://arstechnica. com/science/2020/07/nasas-inspector-general-report-roasts-lockheed-martin-for-orion-fees/ (accessed August 19, 2025).

31. NASA. December 5, 2019. "NASA Commits to Long-Term Artemis Missions with Orion Production Contract." *NASA.* https://www .nasa.gov/news-release/nasa-commits-to-long-term-artemis-missions-with-orion-production-contract/ (accessed August 19, 2025).

32. NASA Office of Inspector General. October 10, 2023. *IG-24-001: NASA's Management of the Space Launch System Stages Contract.* https://oig.nasa.gov/wp-content/uploads/2023/10/ig-24-001.pdf (accessed August 19, 2025).

33. NASA. October 16, 2019. "NASA Commits to Future Artemis Missions with More SLS Rocket Engines." *NASA.* https://www.nasa .gov/news-release/nasa-commits-to-future-artemis-missions-with-more-sls-rocket-engines/ (accessed August 19, 2025).

34. NASA. April 3, 2024. "NASA Selects Companies to Advance Moon Mobility for Artemis Missions." *NASA.* https://www.nasa .gov/news-release/nasa-selects-companies-to-advance-moon-mobility-for-artemis-missions/ (accessed August 19, 2025).

35. Foust, J. May 26, 2020. "Boeing Warns SLS Employees of Potential Layoffs." *SpaceNews.* https://spacenews.com/boeing-warns-sls-employees-of-potential-layoffs/ (accessed August 19, 2025).

36. NASA. July 6, 2021. "NASA Extends Hubble Space Telescope Science Operations Contract." *NASA.* https://www.nasa.gov/ news-release/nasa-extends-hubble-space-telescope-science-operations-contract/ (accessed August 19, 2025).

37. NASA. November 18, 2020. "NASA Selects Commercial Small-sat Data Acquisition Contractors." *NASA*. https://www.nasa.gov/news-release/nasa-selects-commercial-smallsat-data-acquisition-contractors/ (accessed August 19, 2025).
38. NASA. July 25, 2024. "NASA Sets Coverage of Firefly's First Robotic Commercial Moon Landing." *NASA*. https://www.nasa.gov/news-release/nasa-sets-coverage-of-fireflys-first-robotic-commercial-moon-landing/ (accessed August 19, 2025).
39. Marquette University Law School. January 23, 2025. "National Survey Finds Overall Approval of Trump Immigration Policies, Disapproval on Tariffs, Economy." *Marquette University News Center*. https://www.marquette.edu/news-center/2025/new-law-poll-national-survey-finds-overall-approval-trump-immigration-policies-disapproval-on-tariffs-economy.php (accessed August 19, 2025).
40. NASA. September 24, 2020. "NASA Investigation Uncovers Cause of Two Science Mission Launch Failures." *NASA*. https://www.nasa.gov/news-release/nasa-investigation-uncovers-cause-of-two-science-mission-launch-failures/ (accessed August 19, 2025).
41. U.S. Securities and Exchange Commission. August 6, 2021. "SEC Charges Company with Fraudulent Cryptocurrency Offering." Press Release 2021-124. https://www.sec.gov/newsroom/press-releases/2021-124 (accessed August 19, 2025).
42. NASA Office of Inspector General. November 19, 2019. *IG-20-005: NASA's Management of the Artemis Missions and Orion Program*. https://oig.nasa.gov/wp-content/uploads/2024/02/IG-20-005.pdf (accessed August 19, 2025).

About the Author

Jeff Nosanov is a seasoned space industry expert and proposal strategist with over a decade and a half of experience working within and alongside NASA. He has contributed to mission development at NASA's Jet Propulsion Laboratory, Johns Hopkins Applied Physics Laboratory, and NASA Headquarters, supporting a wide range of science and exploration initiatives.

Jeff served as the proposal manager for NASA's Interstellar Mapping and Acceleration Probe (IMAP) mission, scheduled to launch in 2025. His leadership was critical in securing this flagship mission, which will study the boundary of the heliosphere and the interactions between our solar system and the interstellar medium.

In his career, Jeff has helped win over $2 billion in funded government proposals, supporting space missions, advanced technology development, and defense-related programs. He is a three-time recipient of the NASA Innovative Advanced Concepts (NIAC) award for bold mission concepts ranging from solar sails to lunar exploration and interstellar precursor probes.

Jeff is also the first person in the United States to earn an LLM in Space and Telecommunications Law, combining legal, technical, and strategic insight into how space programs operate and how companies can align with them. He has served in senior business development roles at Amazon Web Services, where he supported major aerospace and defense initiatives, including billion-dollar satellite procurements.

Through his consulting firm Orbital Velocity (www.orbitalvelocity.space), Jeff helps start-ups, research institutions, and established contractors navigate the complex landscape of government funding and NASA procurement. His passion lies in translating visionary ideas into funded, executable programs that push the boundaries of exploration and innovation.

Index

Antares, 16
Apathy, 100–101
Apollo program, 3, 88
    economic context, 6–7
    innovation, 5–6
    landmark contractors, 3–4
    partnership, 5–6
    political context, 6–7
    prime contractors, 3–4
    Space Shuttle program, 7–11
Artemis Human Landing System
    Contract, 44–45
Artemis program, 20–23, 83
    Accords framework, 65–66
    challenges, 58
    contract management, 64–65
    economic significance, 66–67
    future perspective, 66–67
    future prospects, 59–61
    international framework, 59
    landmark contracts, 23–25
    Orion Spacecraft contracts, 62
    post mission analysis, 57
    prime contractor, 62
    roadmap, 56–58
    Space Launch System (SLS)
        contracts, 62–63
    timeline adjustments, 58
    Trump administration, 67–72
Astrophysics Division, 73

Blue Ghost, 78–79
Blue Origin, 44–45
Boeing, 12, 18, 19

Challenger disaster, 9–11
Challenges, NASA, 99
    American apathy, 100–101
    China, 99–100
    European doubt, 101–102

fraudulent and disingenuous actors,
    102–104
single private actor, overreliance,
    104–106
Chandra X-ray Observatory, 73–74
Collaboration, 85–86
    financial assistance with, 31–33
    industry, 3, 11
    public-private, 7, 13, 15, 25
Columbia Disaster Claim, 50–51
Commercial Crew Development
    (CCDev), 18
Commercial Crew Integrated
    Capability (CciCap), 18
Commercial Crew Program, 15,
    18–20, 45–46
Commercial Crew Transportation
    Capability (CCtCap)
    contracts, 18
Commercial experiments, 10–11
Commercial Lunar Payload Services
    (CLPS), 22
Commercial Lunar Payload Services
    (CLPS) initiative, 77–78
    commercial space exploration
        model, 80–81
    Firefly Aerospace Blue Ghost
        mission, 78–79
    future missions, 80
    Intuitive Machines (IM-2 mission),
        79
    private equity, 80–81
Commercial Orbital Transportation
    Services (COTS), 14–18
Commercial renaissance, 84–85
Commercial Resupply Services (CRS),
    15, 17–18
Commercial SmallSat Data
    Acquisition Program, 74, 77
Commercial Space Act, 14
Commercial spaceflight revolution, 14

Commercial Space Launch Act, 1984, 9
Competitive procurements, 13
Contract disputes, 44
Contract protests, 51–52
Cooperative agreements, 13, 31–33
Cooperative Research and Development Agreements (CRADAs), 36–38
Cost-plus contracting model, 6
Cost-plus contracts, 28
Cost-plus-fixed fee, 2
Cygnus, 16

Discovery program, 13
Dragonfly missions, 76

Earth Science Division, 74
Earth system, 88–89

FAR-based contracts, 18
Financial assistance
    with collaboration, 31–33
    Grants, 29–31
Firefly Aerospace Blue Ghost mission, 78–79
Firm-fixed-price (FFP) contracts, 28
Fixed-price contracts, 13, 17, 18, 21
Funded SAA, 34

GOES-R Weather Satellite Contract, 52–53
Grants, 29–31

Heat shield materials, 3
Heliophysics Division, 75
High-profile NASA contract award protests, 52
Hubble Space Telescope, 73
Human exploration
    Artemis missions, 56–61
    components, 55–56
    technical architecture, 55–56
Human Landing System (HLS), 21, 22
100 orbital launches, 100
100-year space plan, 99
Hybrid partnership model, 24

Industry collaboration, 3, 11
Integrated circuits (ICs), 2
International SAA, 34–35
International Space Station (ISS), 11, 12
Interstellar, 87–88
ISS Resupply Services Contract, 46–47

James Webb Space Telescope (JWST), 74
Johnson Space Center, 14

Kistler Aerospace, 49–50

Lucy Mission Launch Contract, 48–49
Lunar Module (LM), 4

Mars, 90
Mars Sample Return (MSR), 76
Martin Marietta, 8
Microelectronics industry, 2
Monopolistic behavior, 104
Moon, 89
Morton Thiokol, 8

NASA Authorization Act, 1957, 53
NASA Centennial challenges program, 14
National Advisory Committee for Aeronautics (NACA), 1
Next Space Technologies for Exploration Partnerships (NextSTEP) Appendix R program, 71
Nonreimbursable SAA, 34
North American Rockwell, 7–8

Orbital Sciences Corporation, 16
Orion, 21, 57
Orion Spacecraft contracts, 62
"Other Transaction" agreements, 10
Overreliance, 104–106

Pay-for-performance approach, 16
Performance- based contract, 12
Planetary Science Division, 76

PlanetSpace, 46–47
Policy changes, 9
Prime contractor, 2, 4–5
Prize competitions, 41–43
Procurement contracts, 27–29
Project Mercury, 1–3
Public–private collaboration, 7
Public-private partnerships, 77–82
Public–private partnerships, 13, 15, 25

Reimbursable SAA, 34
Reorganization, 90–93
Robust exploration, 81
Rocketdyne, 8
Rocketplane Kistler (RpK), 16
Rosalind Franklin Mars rover, 101

Science Mission Directorate (SMD), 72
    Astrophysics Division, 73
    Chandra X-ray Observatory, 73–74
    Commercial SmallSat Data
        Acquisition Program, 74
    Dragonfly missions, 76
    Earth Science Division, 74
    Heliophysics Division, 75
    Hubble Space Telescope, 73
    James Webb Space Telescope
        (JWST), 74
    Mars Sample Return (MSR), 76
    overview, 73
    Planetary Science Division, 76
    Solar Dynamics Observatory
        (SDO), 75

Starlab missions, 76–77
    Terra spacecraft, 74
Shared responsibility, 21
Sierra Nevada, 45–46
Small Business Innovation Research
    (SBIR/STTR) contracts,
    39–41
Solar Dynamics Observatory (SDO),
    75
Sole-Source Contract, 49–50
Space Act Agreements (SAAs), 14, 16,
    17, 33–36
Space commerce, 9
Space economy, 24
Spacehab, 50–51
Space Launch System (SLS), 21, 55,
    62–63
Space Policy Directive-1 (2017), 23
Space Race, 1, 86–87
Space science missions, 10
Space Shuttle Columbia, 8
Space Shuttle Main Engine, 10
Space Shuttle program, 7–11
Space Shuttle Spacelab module, 10
Space Station Freedom, 10
SpaceX, 16, 18, 19, 20, 21, 48–49
Starlab missions, 76–77
Substantial involvement, 31–32

Terra spacecraft, 74
Trump administration, 67–72, 83

United Space Alliance (USA), 9

X-33 program, 13

www.ingramcontent.com/pod-product-compliance
Lightning Source LLC
Chambersburg PA
CBHW061333220326
41599CB00026B/5165